Contents

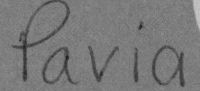

Phonics Centers
Level C

What's Great About This Book?

Centers are a wonderful, fun way for students to practice important skills. The 12 centers in this book are self-contained and portable. Students may work at a table or even on the floor. Once you've made the centers, they're ready to use at any time.

Everything You Need

- Teacher direction page

  How to make the center

  Description of student task

- Full-color materials needed for the center
- Reproducible student activity sheets

Using the Center

The centers are intended for skill practice, not to introduce skills. It is important to model the use of each center before students do the task independently.

Questions to Consider

- Will students select a center, or will you assign the center?
- Will there be a specific block of time for centers, or will the centers be used throughout the day?
- Where will you place the centers for easy access by students?
- What procedure will students use when they need help with the center tasks?
- Where will students store completed work?
- How will you track the tasks and centers completed by each student?

Making an Envelope Center

Materials

- 9" x 12" (23 x 30.5 cm) large envelopes
- scissors
- marking pens
- glue or two-sided tape

Steps to Follow

1. Remove and laminate the center cover page. Glue or tape it to the front of the envelope.

2. Remove and laminate the student direction page. Glue or tape it to the back of the envelope.

3. Remove, laminate, and cut apart the manipulatives (sorting mats, task cards, pockets, etc.) and place them in the envelope.

4. Reproduce copies of the student activity sheet and place them in the envelope.

Note: If a center contains small pieces such as letter cards, place them in a smaller envelope within the larger envelope.

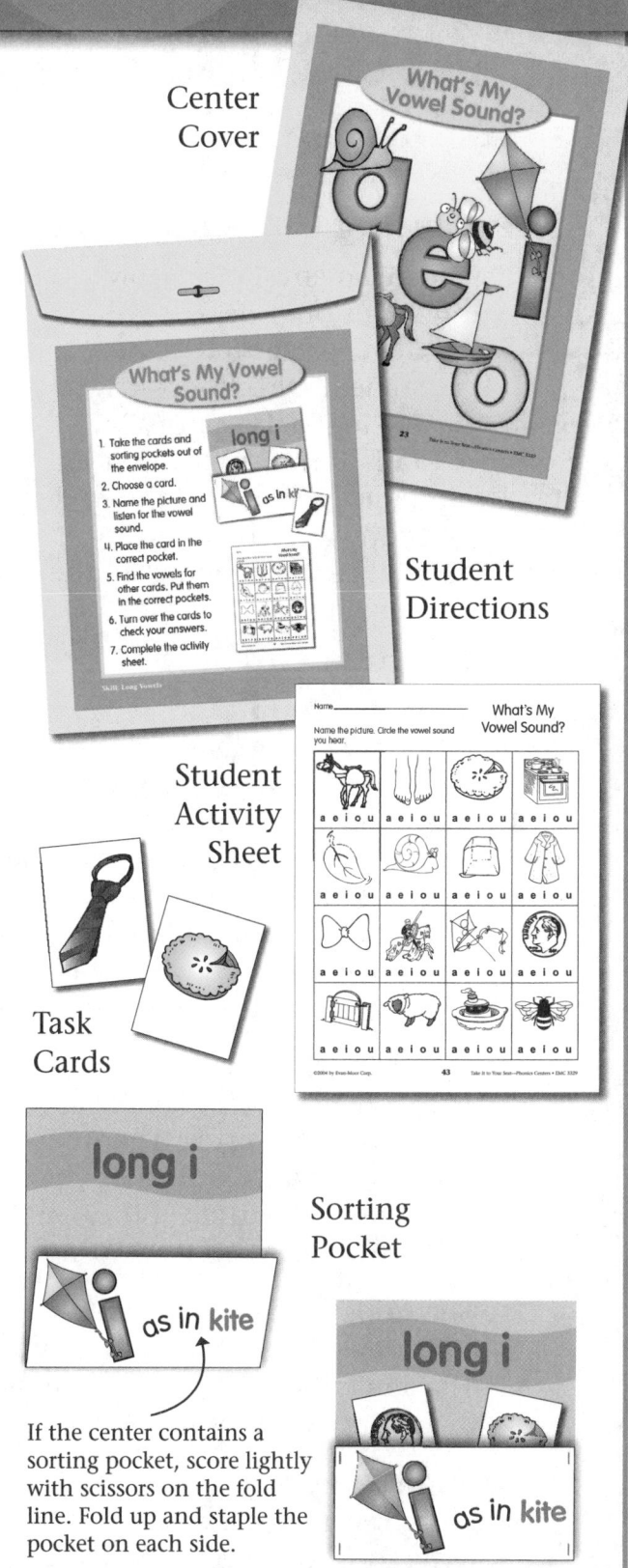

Center Cover

Student Directions

Student Activity Sheet

Task Cards

Sorting Pocket

If the center contains a sorting pocket, score lightly with scissors on the fold line. Fold up and staple the pocket on each side.

Long or Short Vowels?

Skill: Long and Short Vowels

Preparing the Center

1. Prepare an envelope following the directions on page 3.
   Cover—page 5
   Student Directions—page 7
   Sorting Mats—pages 9–13
   Task Cards—pages 15–19
2. Reproduce a supply of the student activity sheet on page 21.
3. Place all center materials in the envelope.

Using the Center

In a Small Group

Take one sorting mat and the matching set of word cards. Place the mat and cards faceup on a flat surface. Have students take turns choosing a card, reading the word, and deciding if the vowel sound is long or short. The card is placed in the correct column and row on the sorting mat. Repeat with each of the other two mats.

Independently

The student selects one mat and the matching set of cards. The student sorts the cards by long and short vowels, and then places the cards in the correct column and row on the sorting mat.

The student takes the activity sheet and circles the shape of the card on the mat. The student completes the activity sheet by writing words in the correct boxes.

Self-Checking Key

Word cards have the long or short letter for the vowel sound indicated on the back.

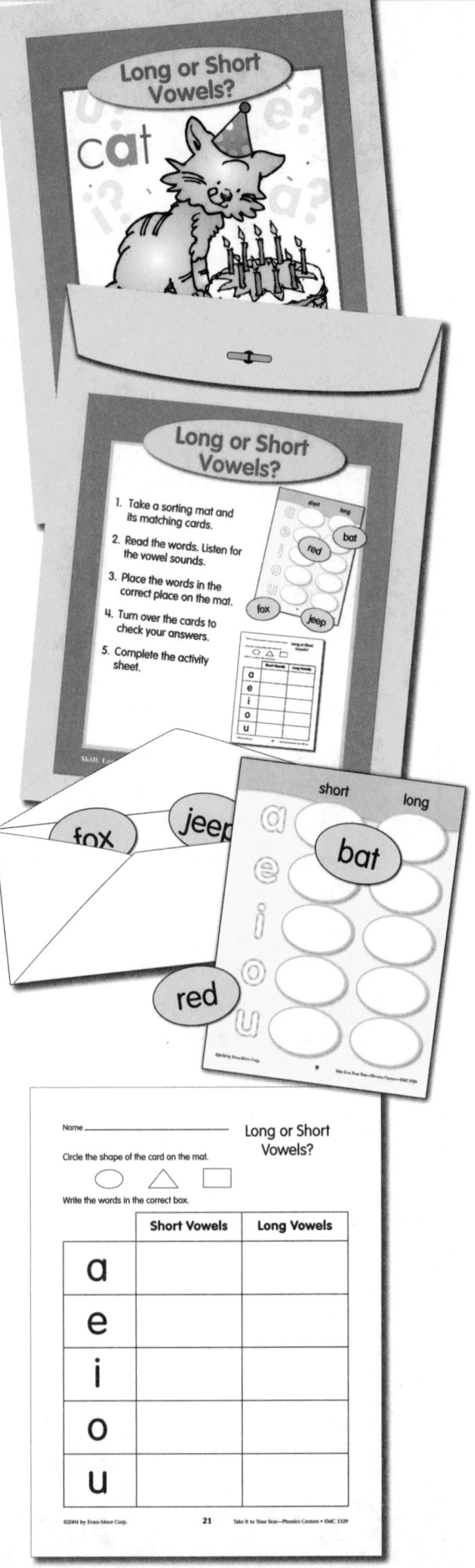

Long or Short Vowels?

cat

cake

6

Long or Short Vowels?

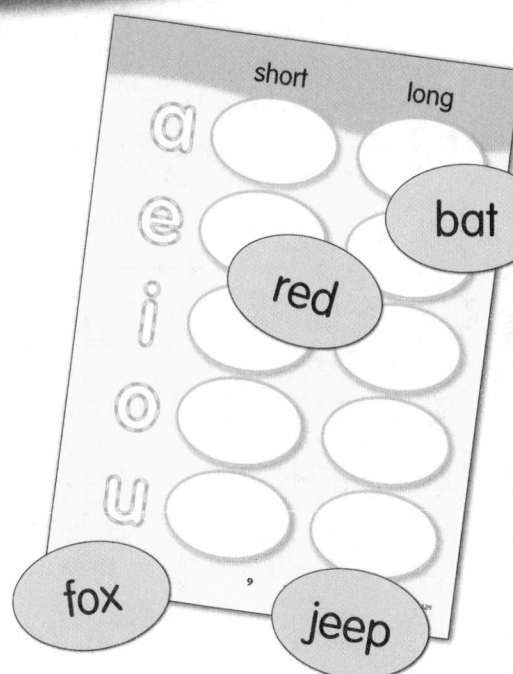

1. Take a sorting mat and its matching cards.

2. Read the words. Listen for the vowel sounds.

3. Place the words in the correct place on the mat.

4. Turn over the cards to check your answers.

5. Complete the activity sheet.

Skill: Long and Short Vowels

8

short   long

 a

 e

 i

 o

 u

9

10

a

e

i

o

u

12

©2004 by Evan-Moor Corp.

short   long

a

e

i

o

u

bat

red

came

jeep

six

fox

like

nose

but

cute

Take It to Your Seat—Phonics Centers • EMC 3329

short

e

long

e

short

o

long

o

long

u

short

a

long

a

short

i

long

i

short

u

and

men

rake

see

him

not

five

most

run

mule

short
e

short
a

long
e

long
a

short
o

short
i

long
o

long
i

long
u

short
u

had	get
made	need
in	on
vine	note
bus	cube

short

e

long

e

short

o

long

o

long

u

short

a

long

a

short

i

long

i

short

u

Name _____

Circle the shape of the card on the mat.

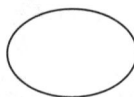  

Write the words in the correct box.

	Short Vowels	Long Vowels
a		
e		
i		
o		
u		

What's My Vowel Sound?

Skill: Long Vowels

Preparing the Center

1. Prepare an envelope following the directions on page 3.
   Cover—page 23
   Student Directions—page 25
   Sorting Pockets—pages 27–31
   Task Cards—pages 31–41
2. Reproduce a supply of the student activity sheet on page 43.
3. Place all center materials in the envelope.

Using the Center

In a Small Group

Place the sorting pockets faceup on a flat surface. Place the picture cards in a small box or bag. Have students take turns choosing a picture card, naming the picture, and listening for the long vowel sound. The picture card is placed in the correct sorting pocket. Continue until all cards have been placed in a pocket.

Independently

The student sorts and places the picture cards in the correct pockets. The student then completes the activity sheet by circling the correct long vowel for each picture.

Self-Checking Key

The back of each picture card has a small letter showing the correct vowel sound.

What's My Vowel Sound?

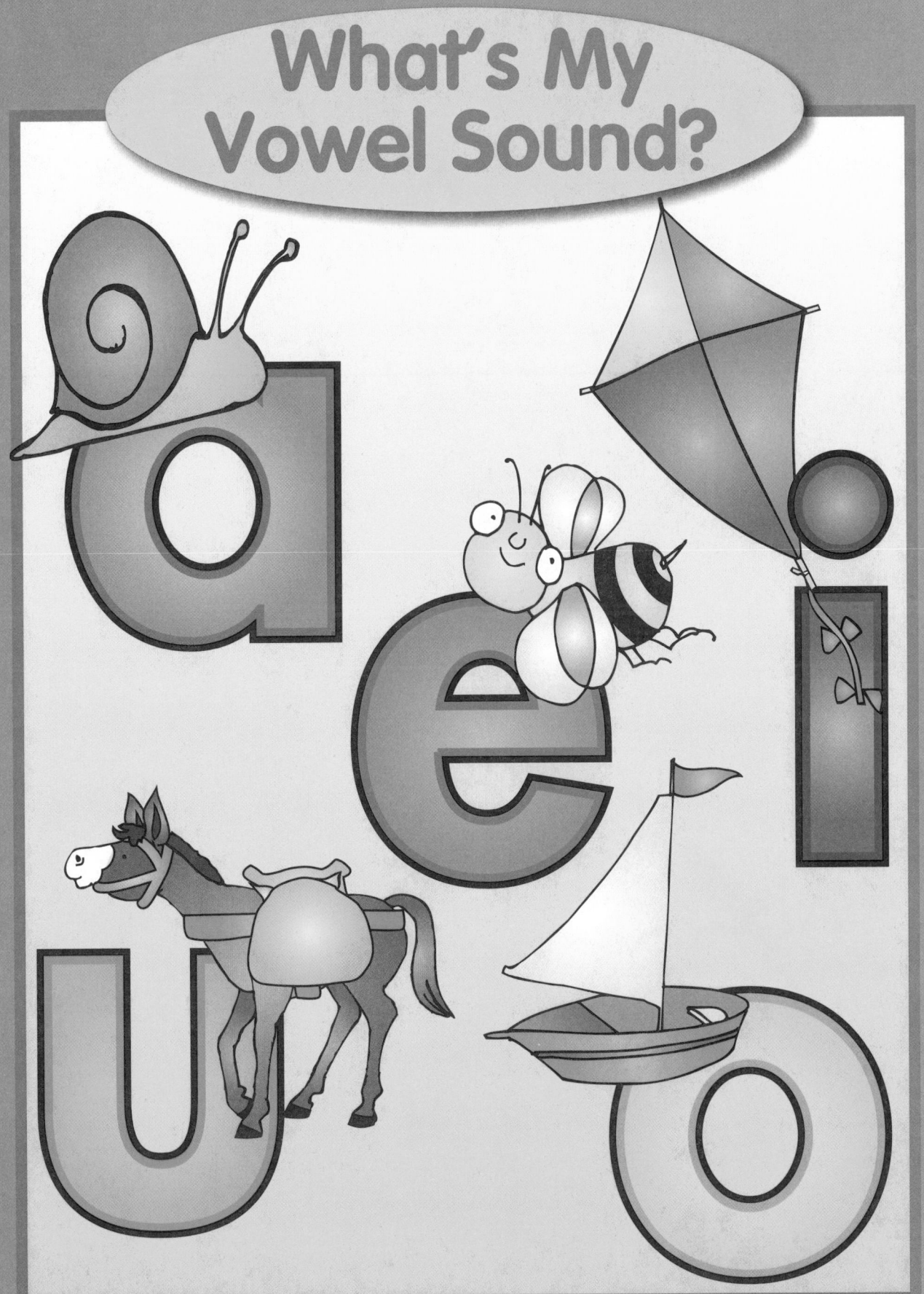

23

24

What's My Vowel Sound?

1. Take the cards and sorting pockets out of the envelope.

2. Choose a card.

3. Name the picture and listen for the vowel sound.

4. Place the card in the correct pocket.

5. Find the vowels for other cards. Put them in the correct pockets.

6. Turn over the cards to check your answers.

7. Complete the activity sheet.

Skill: Long Vowels

26

long a

fold

cut

long e

fold

b as in snail

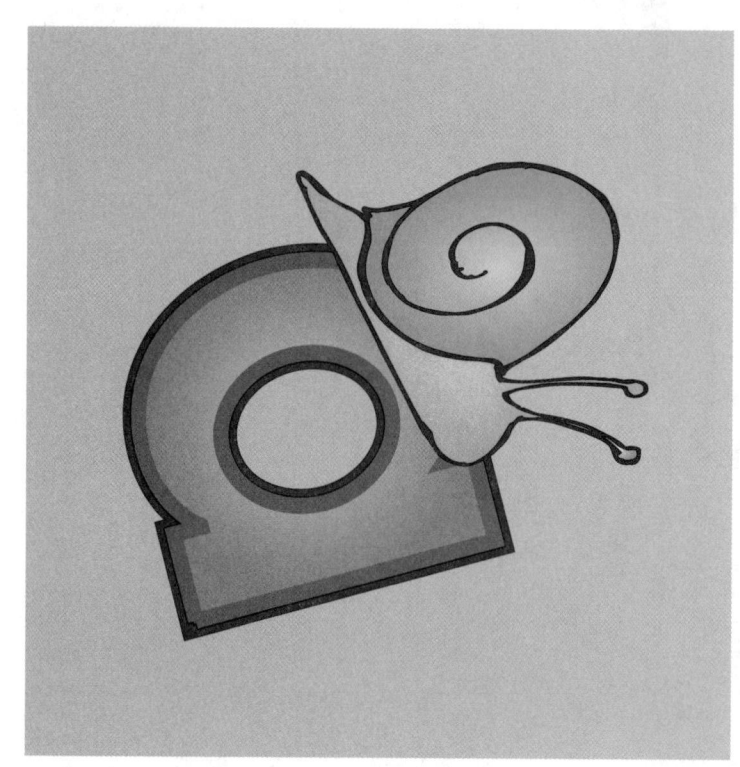

e as in bee

long i

cut

fold

long o

fold

ī as in kite

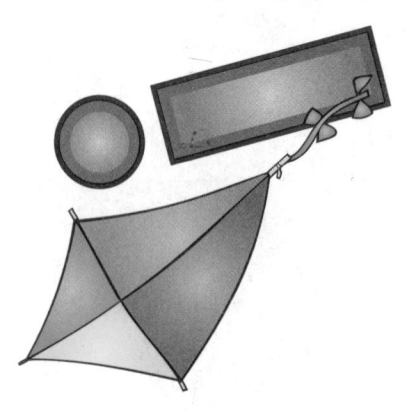

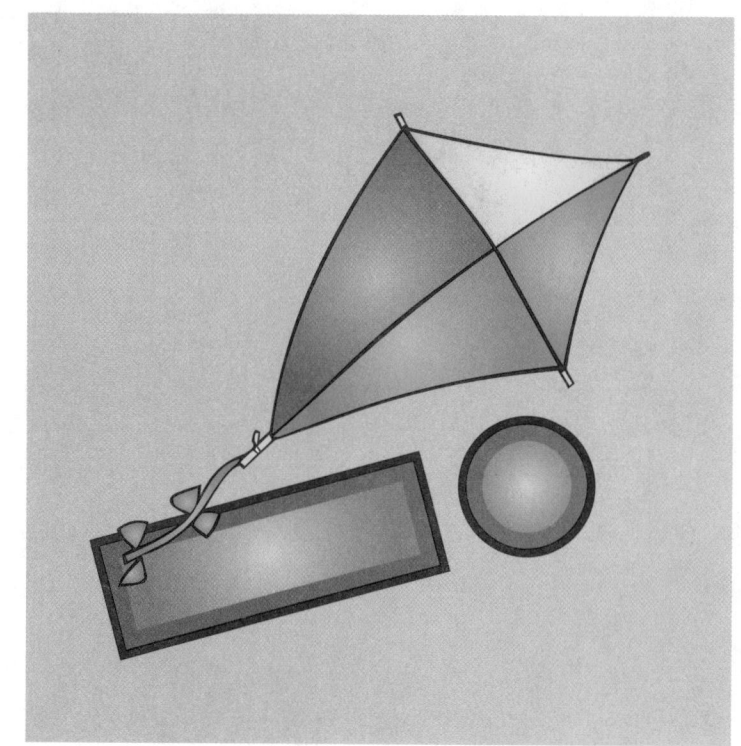

ō as in boat

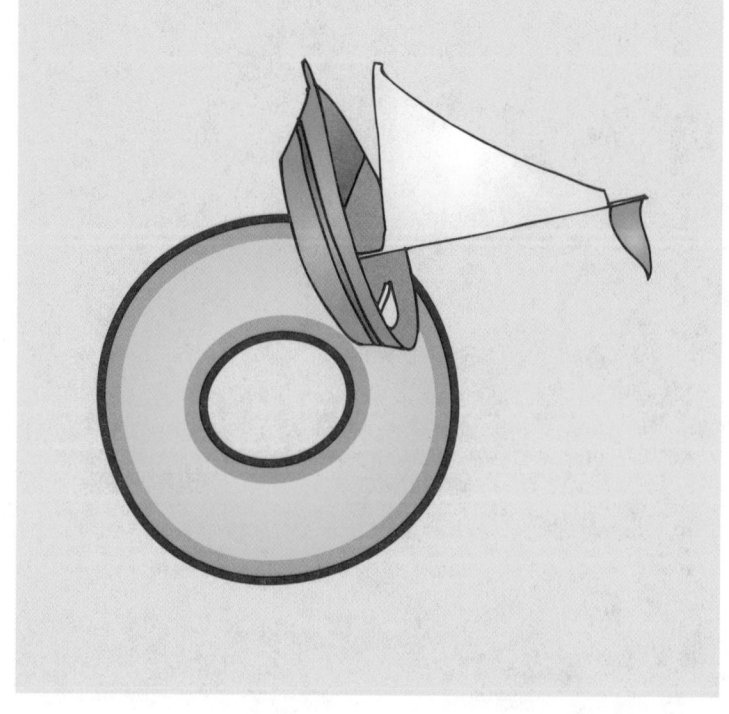

long u

fold

cut

U as in mule

o

e

a

a

a

a

a

a

a

a

a

a

u

u

u

u

u

u

u

u

u

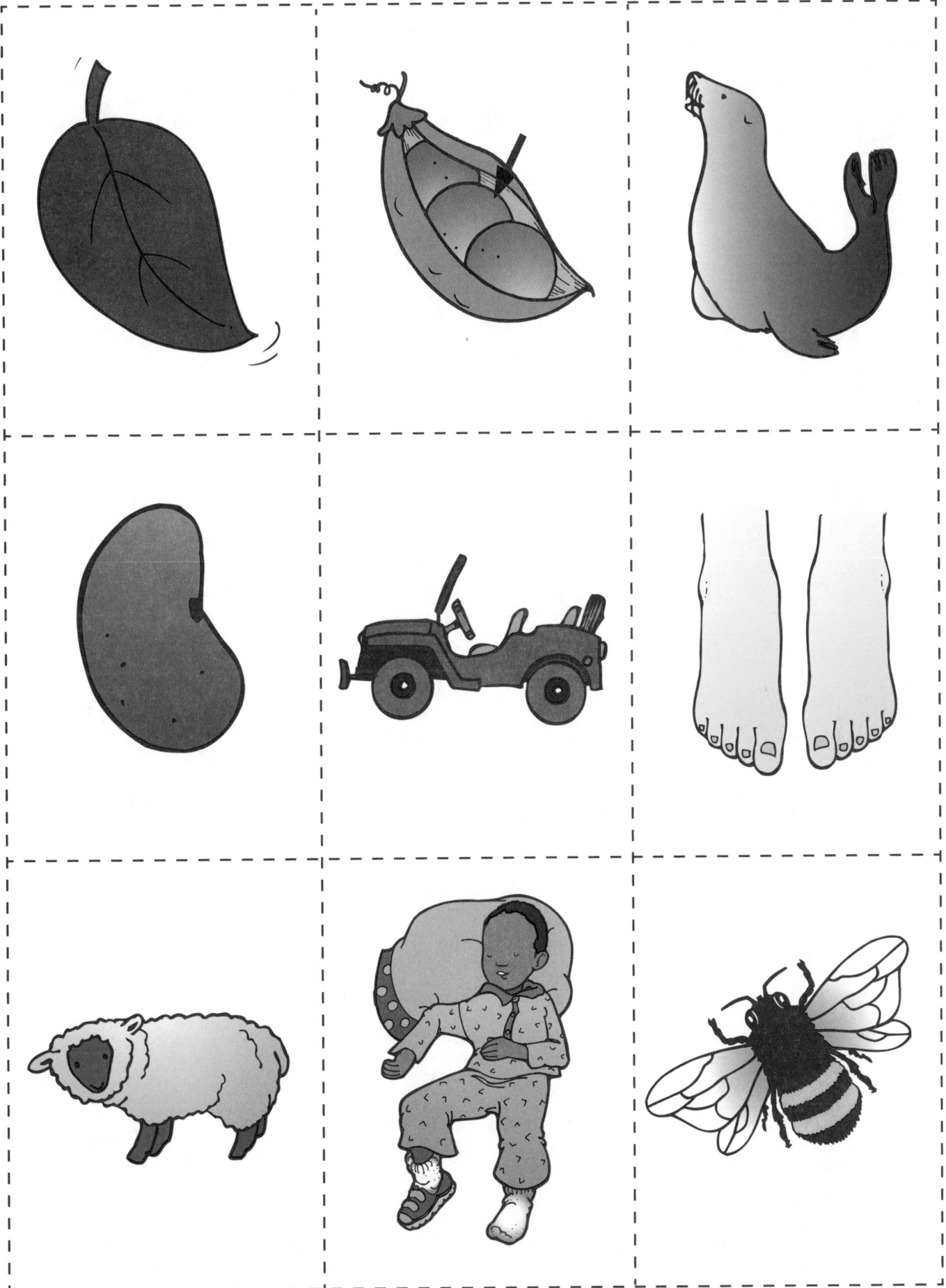

e

e

e

e

e

e

e

e

e

39

i

i

i

i

i

i

i

i

i

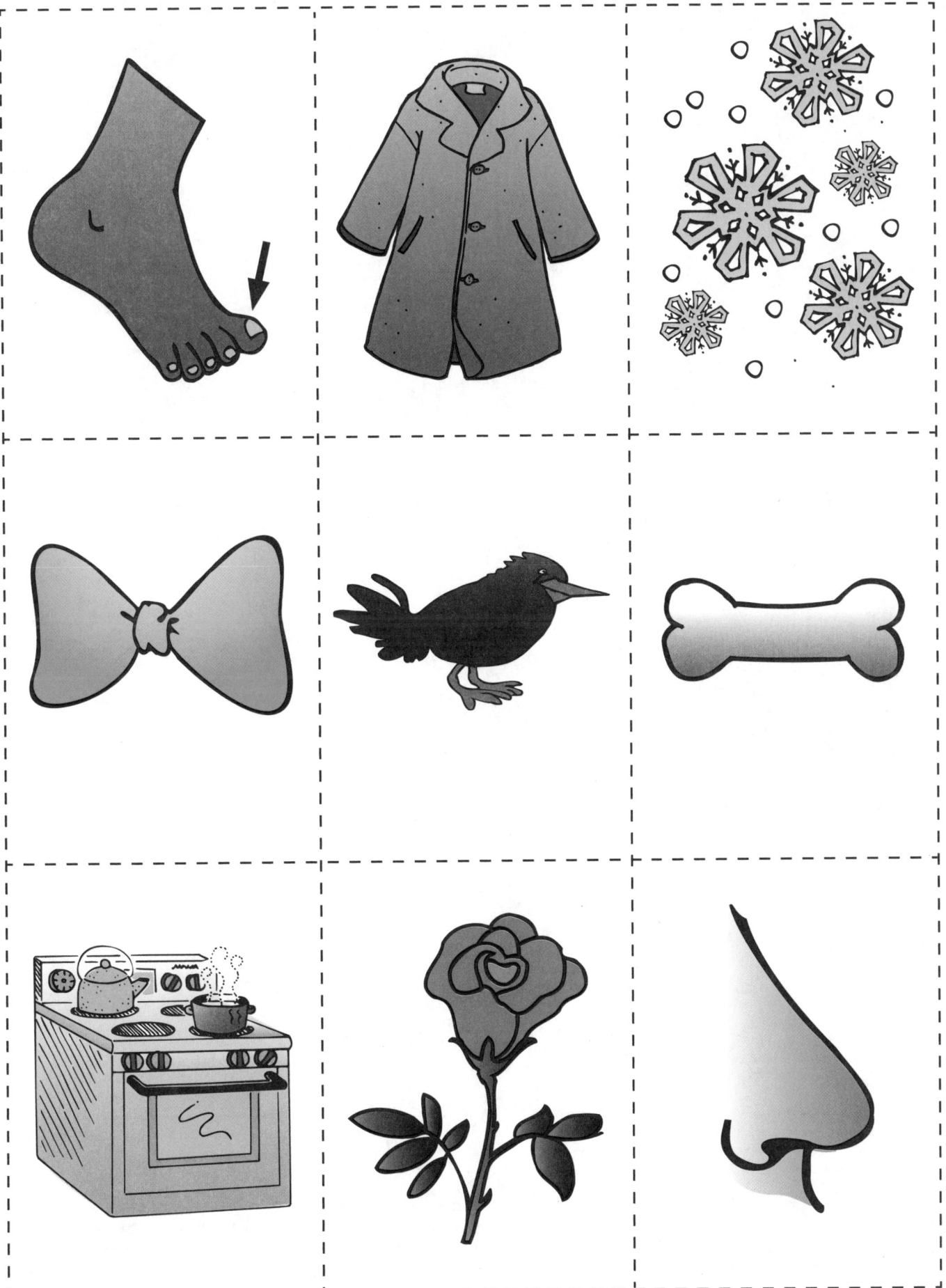

What's My Vowel Sound?

Name the picture. Circle the vowel sound you hear.

a e i o u	a e i o u	a e i o u	a e i o u
a e i o u	a e i o u	a e i o u	a e i o u
a e i o u	a e i o u	a e i o u	a e i o u
a e i o u	a e i o u	a e i o u	a e i o u

Spell It!

Skill: Spelling Vowel Digraphs

Preparing the Center

1. Prepare an envelope following the directions on page 3.
    - Cover—page 45
    - Student Directions—page 47
    - Task Cards—pages 49–57
    - Letter Cards—page 59
2. Reproduce a supply of the student activity sheet on page 61.
3. Place all center materials in the envelope.

Using the Center

In a Small Group

Lay the picture cards faceup on a flat surface. Place the letter cards faceup nearby. Have students take turns choosing a picture card, naming the picture, and finding the letter card that completes the spelling of the word. The letter card is placed in the box on the picture card.

Independently

The student places letter cards on the picture cards to spell each word. The student then completes the activity sheet by circling and writing the missing letters to correctly spell words.

Self-Checking Key

The word is spelled correctly on the back of each picture card.

Spell It!

snail

green
leaf

Snail eats a leaf.

46

Spell It!

1. Choose a picture card and name the picture.

2. Find the letter card that helps spell the word.

3. Turn over the picture cards to check your answers.

4. Complete the activity sheet.

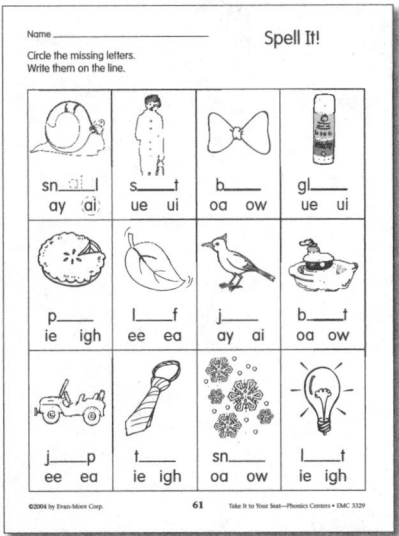

Skill: Spelling Vowel Digraphs

48

sn ___ l

r ___ n

h ___

j ___

snail

rain

hay

jay

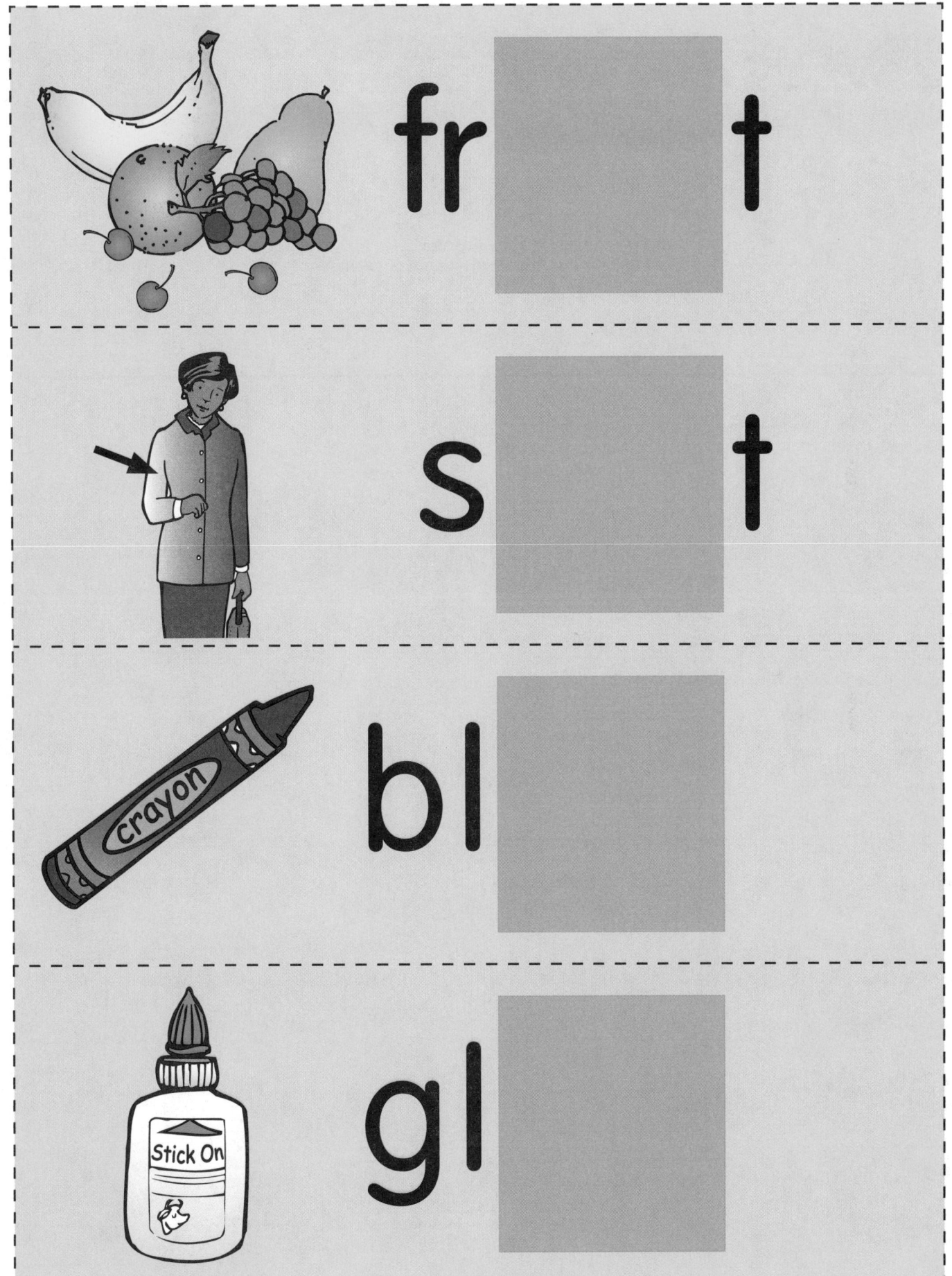

fr [   ] t

s [   ] t

bl [   ]

gl [   ]

Take It to Your Seat—Phonics Centers • EMC 3329

fruit

suit

blue

glue

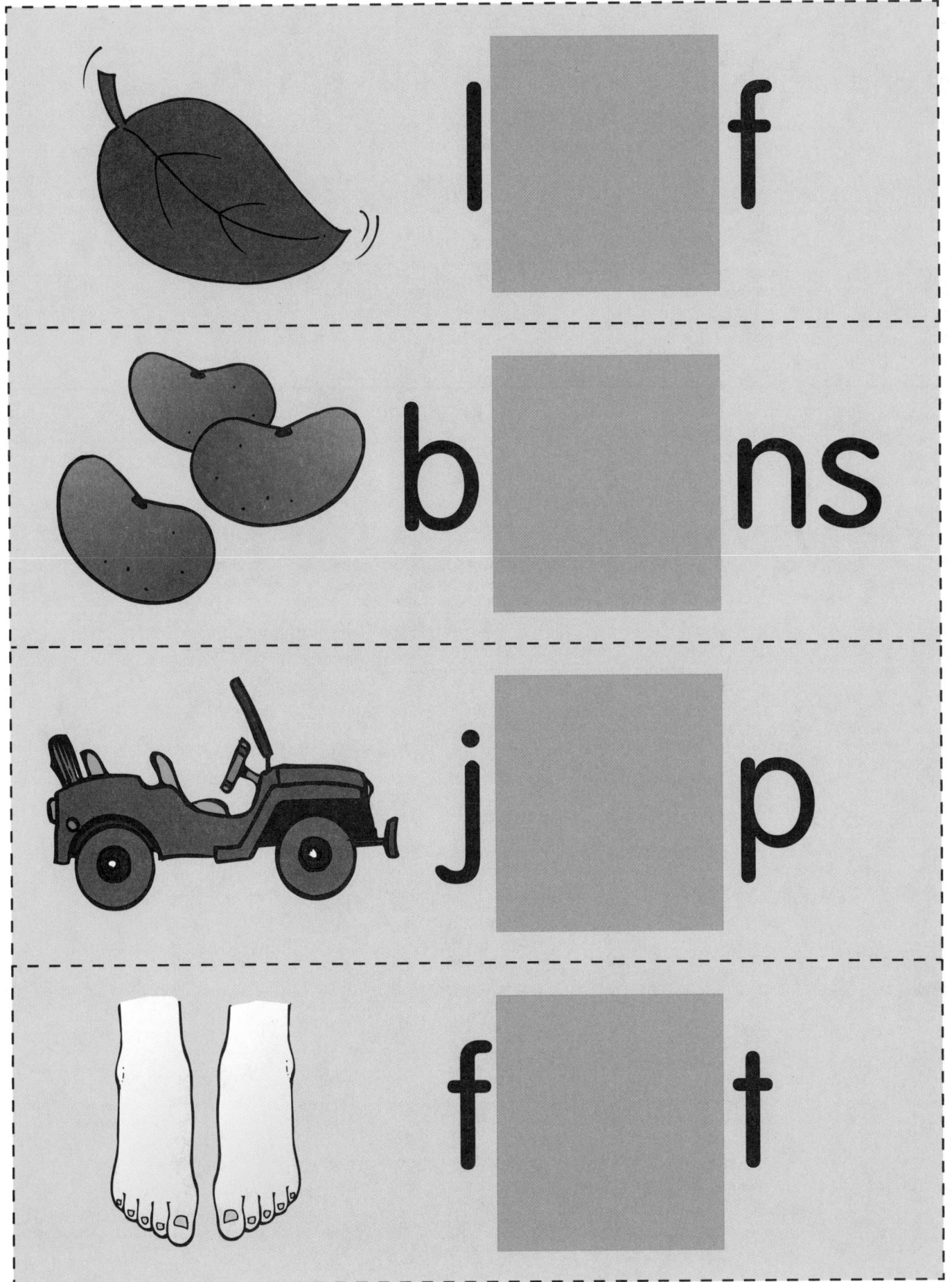

l [ ] f

b [ ] ns

j [ ] p

f [ ] t

leaf

beans

jeep

feet

54

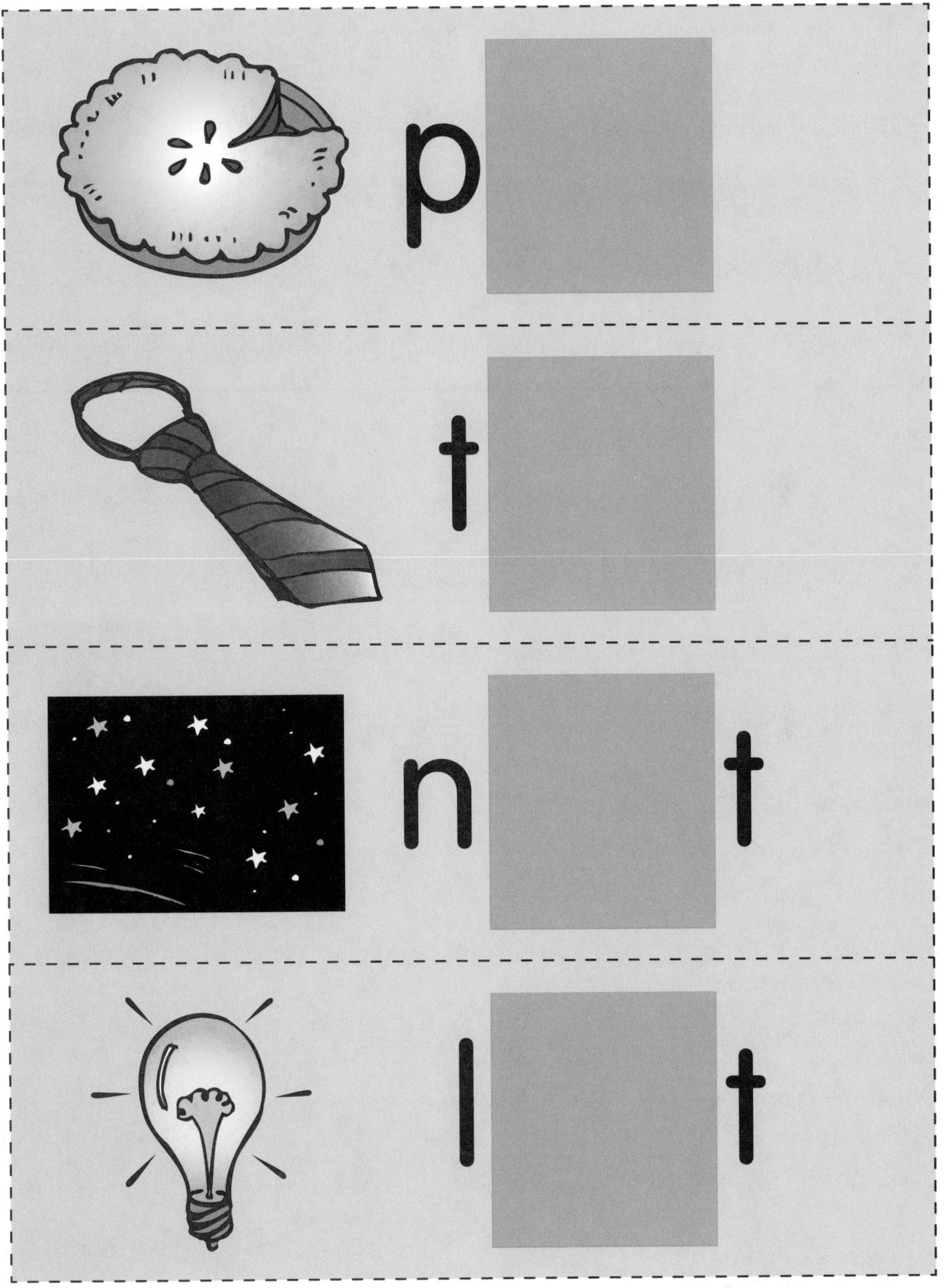

pie

tie

night

light

56

boat

goat

snow

bow

58

ai	ai	ay	ay
ui	ui	ue	ue
ea	ea	ee	ee
ie	ie	igh	igh
oa	oa	ow	ow

Name _____

Circle the missing letters.
Write them on the line.

sn __ai__ l	s ____ t	b ____	gl ____
ay ai	ue ui	oa ow	ue ui
p ____	l ____ f	j ____	b ____ t
ie igh	ee ea	ay ai	oa ow
j ____ p	t ____	sn ____	l ____ t
ee ea	ie igh	oa ow	ie igh

61   Take It to Your Seat—Phonics Centers • EMC 3329

Find the Sound

Skill: Soft and Hard Sounds of *c* and *g*

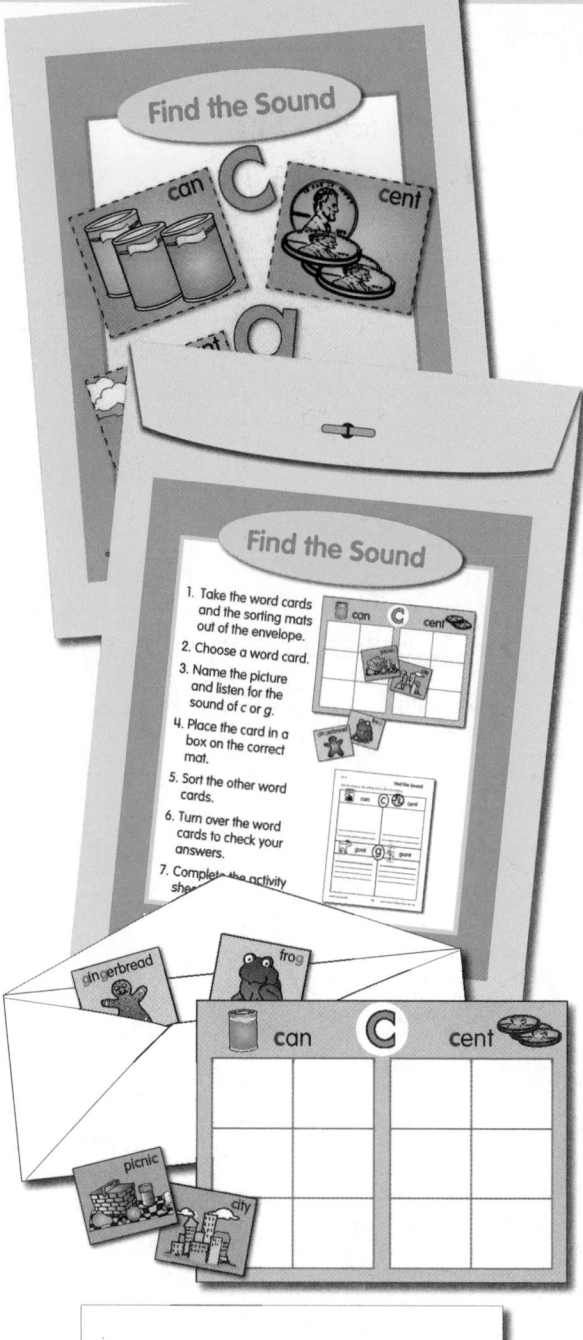

Preparing the Center

1. Prepare an envelope following the directions on page 3.
   - Cover—page 63
   - Student Directions—page 65
   - Sorting Mats—pages 67 and 69
   - Task Cards—pages 71 and 73
2. Reproduce a supply of the student activity sheet on page 75.
3. Place all center materials in the envelope.

Using the Center

In a Small Group

Lay the sorting mats faceup on a flat surface. Place the cards in a small box or bag. Have students take turns choosing a card, reading the word, and deciding on which mat the word belongs. The cards are placed according to the soft or hard *g* and *c* sounds.

Independently

The student places the cards in the correct box on the correct sorting mat. The student then completes the activity sheet by writing the words in the correct boxes.

Self-Checking Key

The word on the back of each picture card matches the word on the sorting mat.

Find the Sound

64

Find the Sound

1. Take the word cards and the sorting mats out of the envelope.

2. Choose a word card.

3. Name the picture and listen for the sound of **c** or **g**.

4. Place the card in a box on the correct mat.

5. Sort the other word cards.

6. Turn over the word cards to check your answers.

7. Complete the activity sheet.

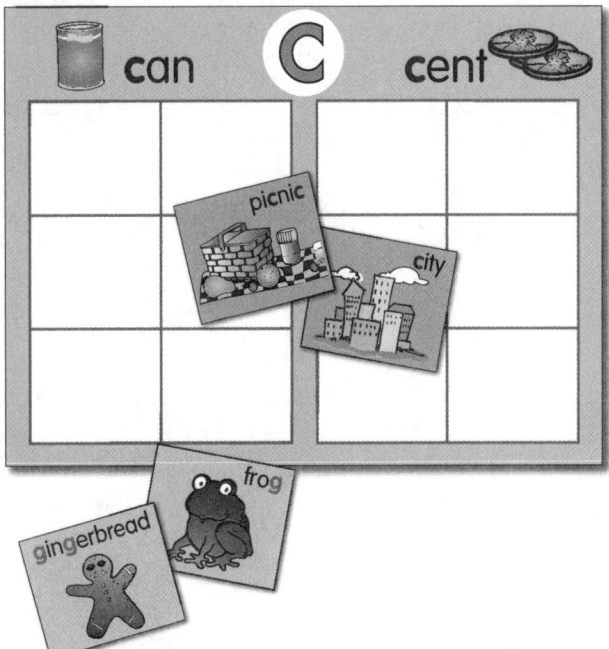

Skill: Soft and Hard Sounds of *c* and *g*

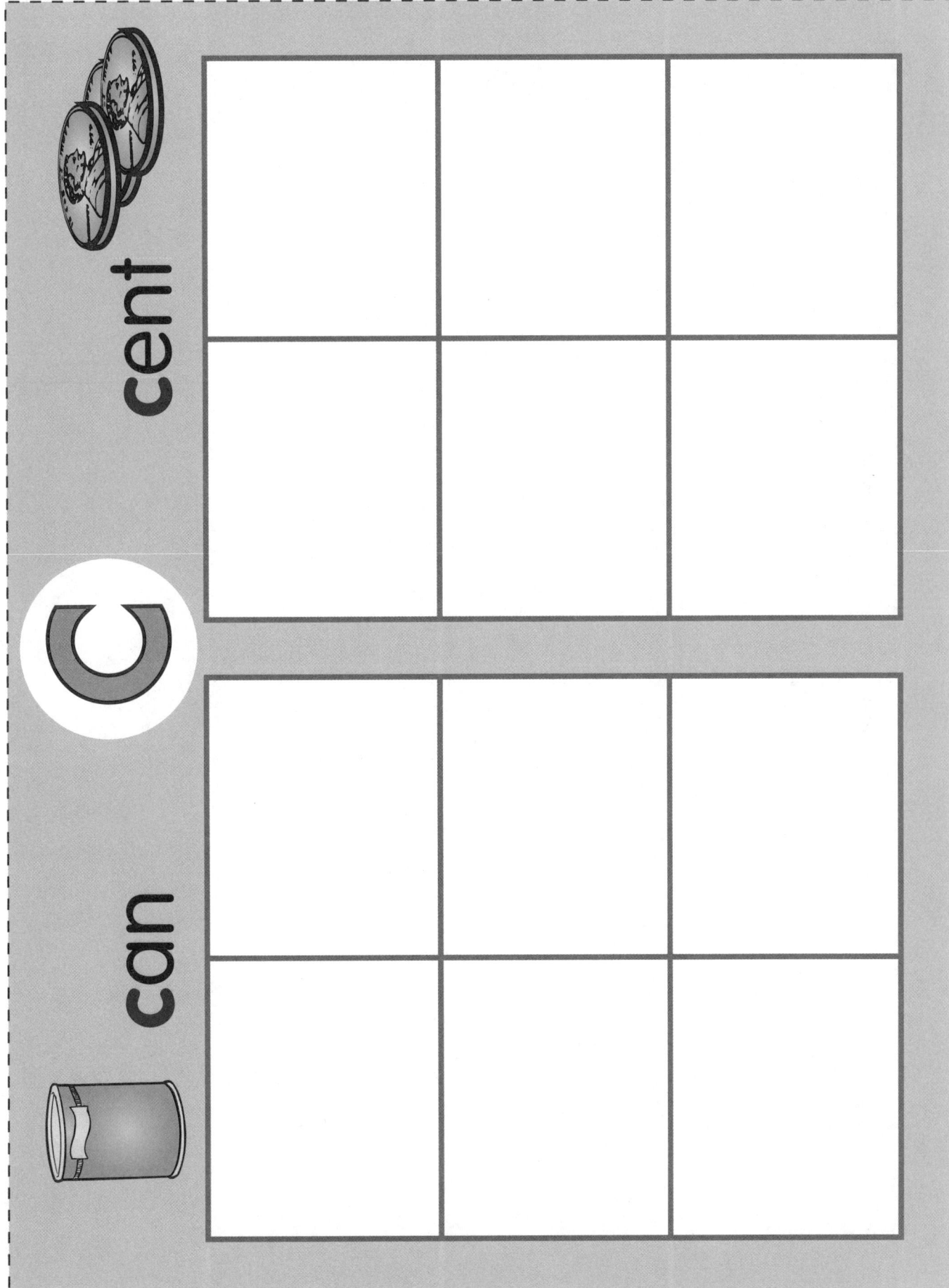

cent

can

68

giant

g

goat

70

cane   corn   comb

coat   cap   picnic

celery   city   fence

face   mice   pencil

       Take It to Your Seat—Phonics Centers • EMC 3329

can

can

can

can

can

can

cent

cent

cent

cent

cent

cent

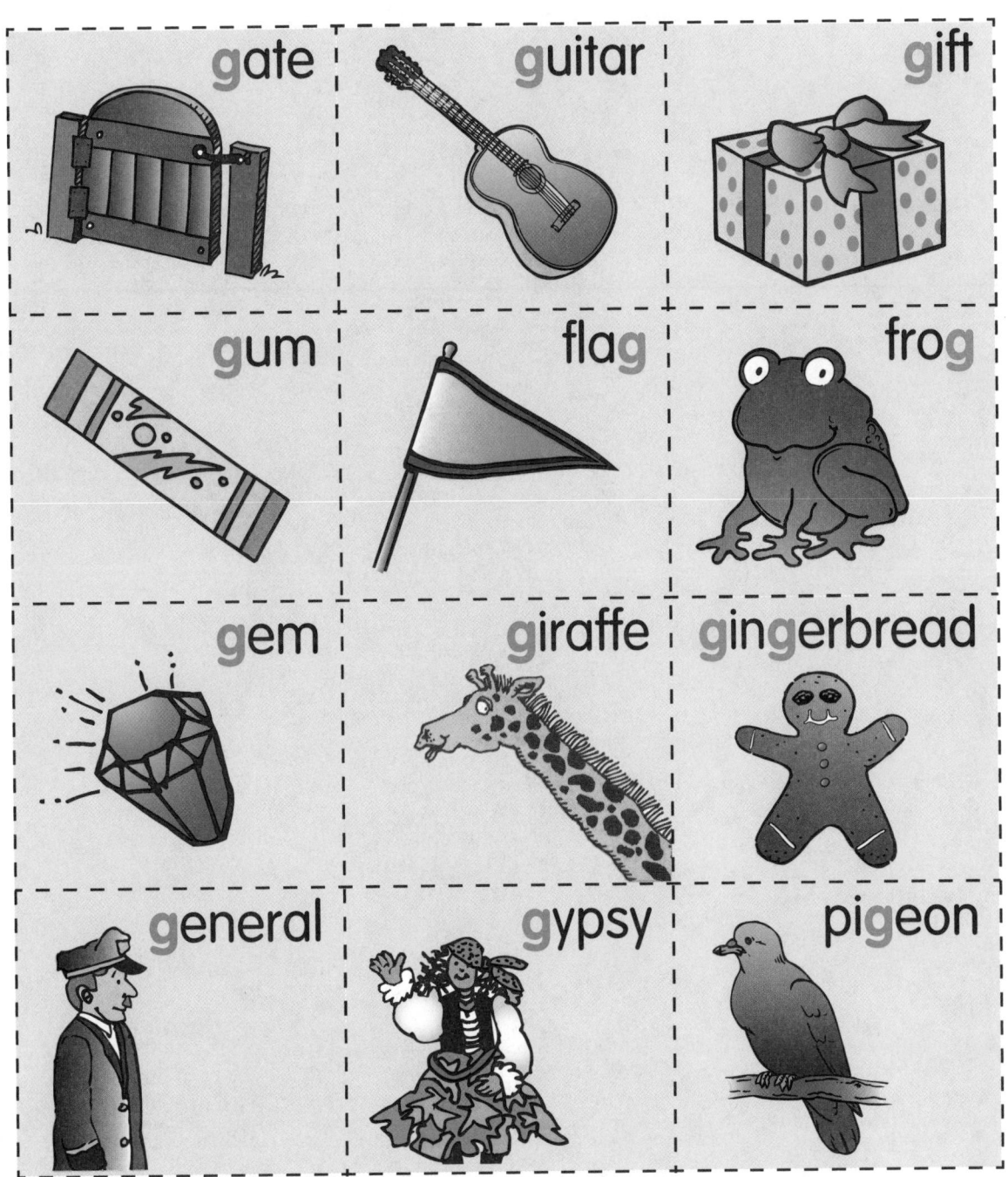

gate

guitar

gift

gum

flag

frog

gem

giraffe

gingerbread

general

gypsy

pigeon

Take It to Your Seat—Phonics Centers • EMC 3329

goat

goat

goat

goat

goat

goat

giant

giant

giant

giant

giant

giant

Find the Sound

Copy the words from the sorting mats in the correct boxes.

can **C** cent

goat **g** giant

What's Missing?

Skill: Consonant Digraphs

Preparing the Center

1. Prepare an envelope following the directions on page 3.
   - Cover—page 77
   - Student Directions—page 79
   - Task Cards—pages 81–87
   - Letter Cards—page 89
2. Reproduce a supply of the student activity sheet on page 91.
3. Place all center materials in the envelope.

Using the Center

In a Small Group
Lay the picture cards faceup on a flat surface. Place the letter cards faceup nearby. Have students take turns choosing a picture card, naming the picture, and finding the letter card that completes the spelling of the word. The letter card is placed in the box on the picture card.

Independently
The student places letter cards on the picture cards to spell each word. The student then completes the activity sheet by writing the missing letters to correctly spell the words.

Self-Checking Key
The complete word is spelled on the back of each picture card.

What's Missing?

wh ale

30 irty

eep

icken

sh   ch   th

78

What's Missing?

1. Choose a picture card and name the picture.

2. Find the letter card that helps spell the word.

3. Turn over the picture cards to check your answers.

4. Complete the activity sheet.

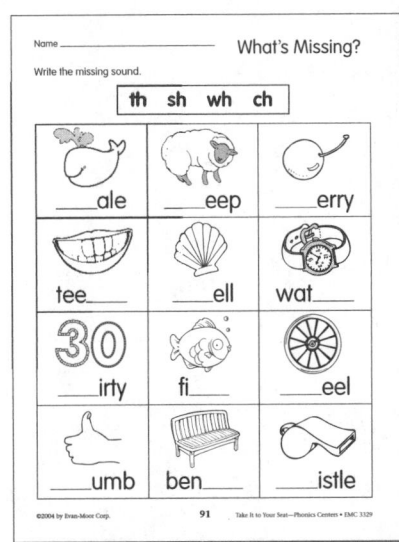

Skill: Consonant Digraphs

80

 ale

 eel

 umb

 irty

Take It to Your Seat—Phonics Centers • EMC 3329

whale

wheel

thumb

thirty

 ell

 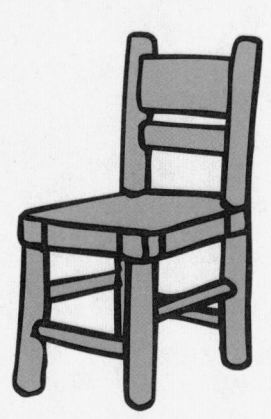eep

air

 icken

 Take It to Your Seat—Phonics Centers • EMC 3329

shell

sheep

chair

chicken

84

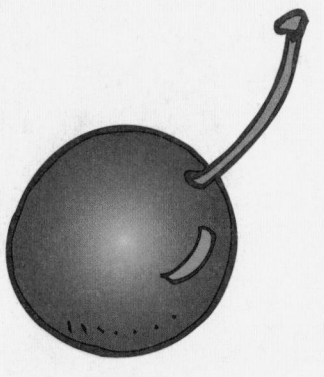erry

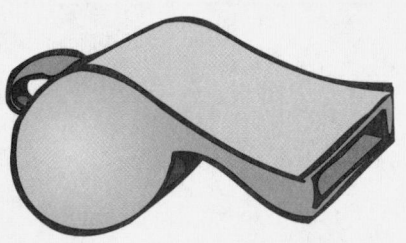istle

ben

wat

 Take It to Your Seat—Phonics Centers • EMC 3329

cherry

whistle

bench

watch

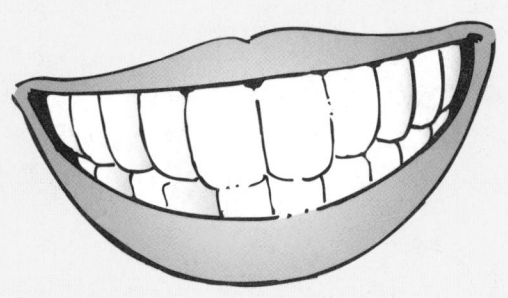 tee

 ba

 fi

 wa

87

teeth

bath

fish

wash

88

th	th	th	th
sh	sh	sh	sh
ch	ch	ch	ch
wh	wh	wh	wh
ch	wh	sh	th

 Take It to Your Seat—Phonics Centers • EMC 3329

90

What's Missing?

Write the missing sound.

th	sh	wh	ch

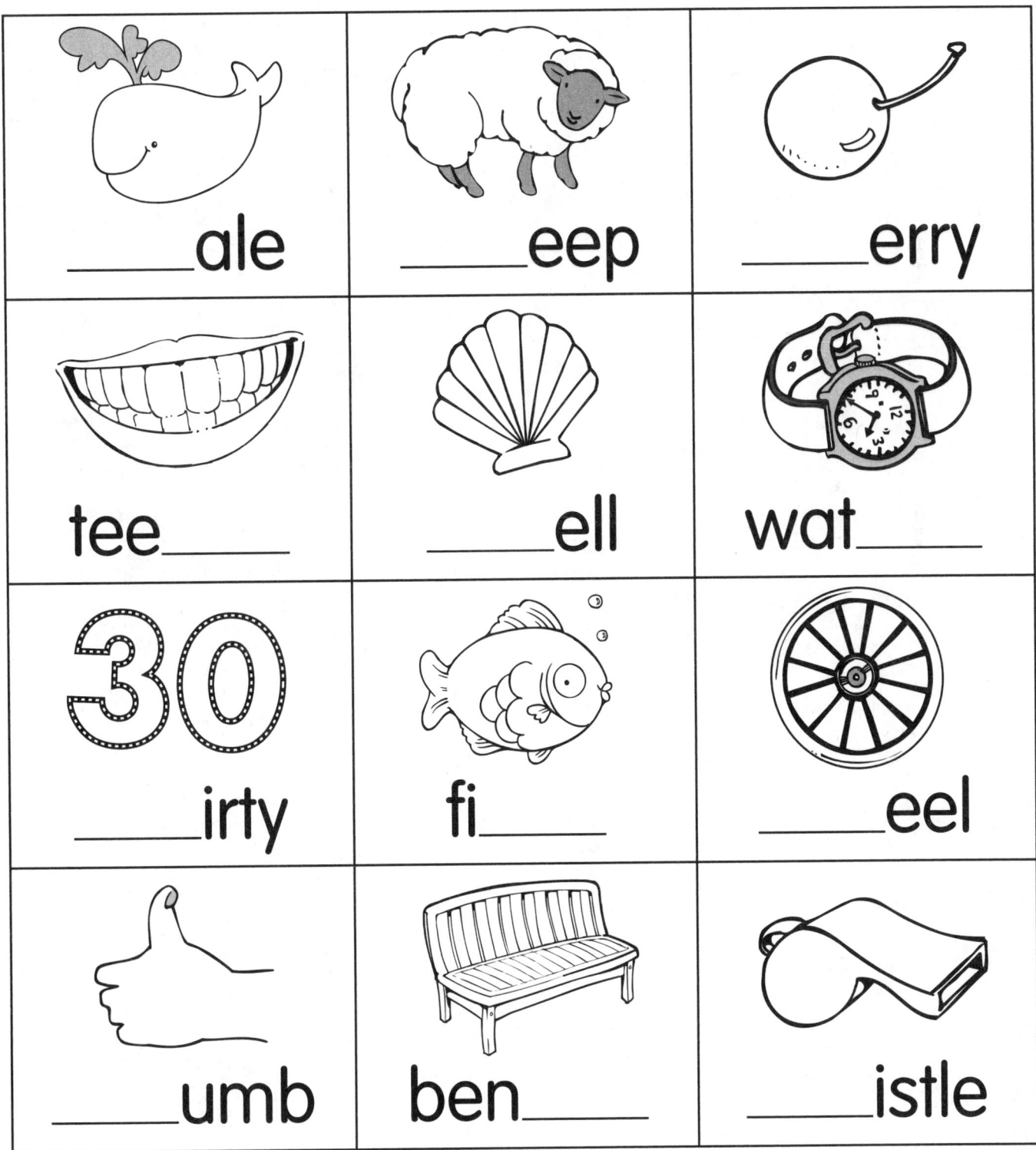

___ale	___eep	___erry
tee___	___ell	wat___
___irty	fi___	___eel
___umb	ben___	___istle

It's a Puzzle

Skill: Initial Consonant Blends

Preparing the Center

1. Prepare an envelope following the directions on page 3.
   - Cover—page 93
   - Student Directions—page 95
   - Task Cards—pages 97–105
2. Reproduce a supply of the student activity sheet on page 107.
3. Place all center materials in the envelope.

Using the Center

In a Small Group

Spread out the letter puzzle pieces faceup on a flat surface. Place the picture pieces in a small box or bag. Have students take turns choosing and naming a puzzle piece, listening for the initial consonant blend. Students match the picture with the correct consonant blend. Continue until each blend is matched to two pictures.

Independently

The student forms sets consisting of a consonant blend and two pictures. The student then writes the missing consonant blends on the activity sheet.

Self-Checking Key

Turn over each set of three pieces. Each correct set has the same colored shape on the back.

92

It's a Puzzle

94

It's a Puzzle

1. Choose a letter and say the sound.

2. Find two pictures whose names begin with that sound. Put the three pieces together.

3. Do the rest of the puzzles.

4. Turn over the puzzles to check your answers.

5. Complete the activity sheet.

Skill: Initial Consonant Blends

96

st

sl

sk

sw

©2004 by Evan-Moor Corp.
Take It to Your Seat—Phonics Centers
EMC 3329

©2004 by Evan-Moor Corp.
Take It to Your Seat—Phonics Centers
EMC 3329

©2004 by Evan-Moor Corp.
Take It to Your Seat—Phonics Centers
EMC 3329

©2004 by Evan-Moor Corp.
Take It to Your Seat—Phonics Centers
EMC 3329

©2004 by Evan-Moor Corp.
Take It to Your Seat—Phonics Centers
EMC 3329

©2004 by Evan-Moor Corp.
Take It to Your Seat—Phonics Centers
EMC 3329

©2004 by Evan-Moor Corp.
Take It to Your Seat—Phonics Centers
EMC 3329

©2004 by Evan-Moor Corp.
Take It to Your Seat—Phonics Centers
EMC 3329

©2004 by Evan-Moor Corp.
Take It to Your Seat—Phonics Centers
EMC 3329

©2004 by Evan-Moor Corp.
Take It to Your Seat—Phonics Centers
EMC 3329

©2004 by Evan-Moor Corp.
Take It to Your Seat—Phonics Centers
EMC 3329

©2004 by Evan-Moor Corp.
Take It to Your Seat—Phonics Centers
EMC 3329

cr

fr

gr

br

It's a Puzzle

Write the missing sound.

cl	cr	dr	fl	fr

gr	pl	sk	st

___ar   ___unk   ___ag

___agon   ___og   ___own

___ab   ___apes   ___ant

Take It to Your Seat—Phonics Centers • EMC 3329

Listen to the End

Skill: Final Consonant Blends

Preparing the Center

1. Prepare an envelope following the directions on page 3.
   Cover—page 109
   Student Directions—page 111
   Sorting Mats—pages 113 and 115
   Task Cards—pages 117 and 119
2. Reproduce a supply of the student activity sheet on page 121.
3. Place all center materials in the envelope.

Using the Center

In a Small Group

Lay the sorting mats faceup on a flat surface. Place the picture cards in a small box or bag. Have students take turns choosing a card, naming the picture, and deciding on which mat to place the card. The cards are placed according to the final consonant blend. There are three cards for each blend.

Independently

The student places the picture cards on the correct sorting mats. The student then draws a picture for each final consonant blend on the activity sheet.

Self-Checking Key

The back of each picture card has a shape the same color as the house on its sorting mat.

Listen to the End

nt

110

Listen to the End

1. Choose a picture card.

2. Name the picture and listen for the ending sound.

3. Place the card on the correct sorting mat.

4. Name the other pictures. Put them on the correct mats.

5. Turn over the picture cards to check your answers.

6. Complete the activity sheets.

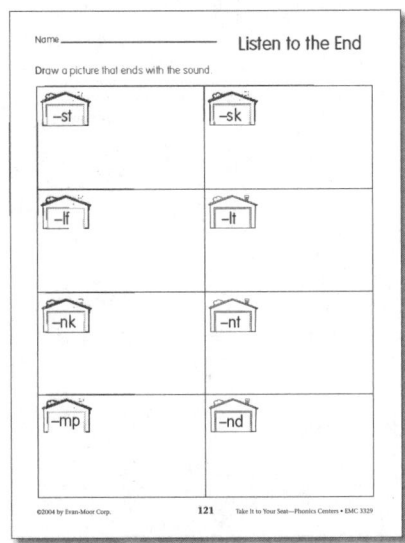

Skill: Final Consonant Blends

112

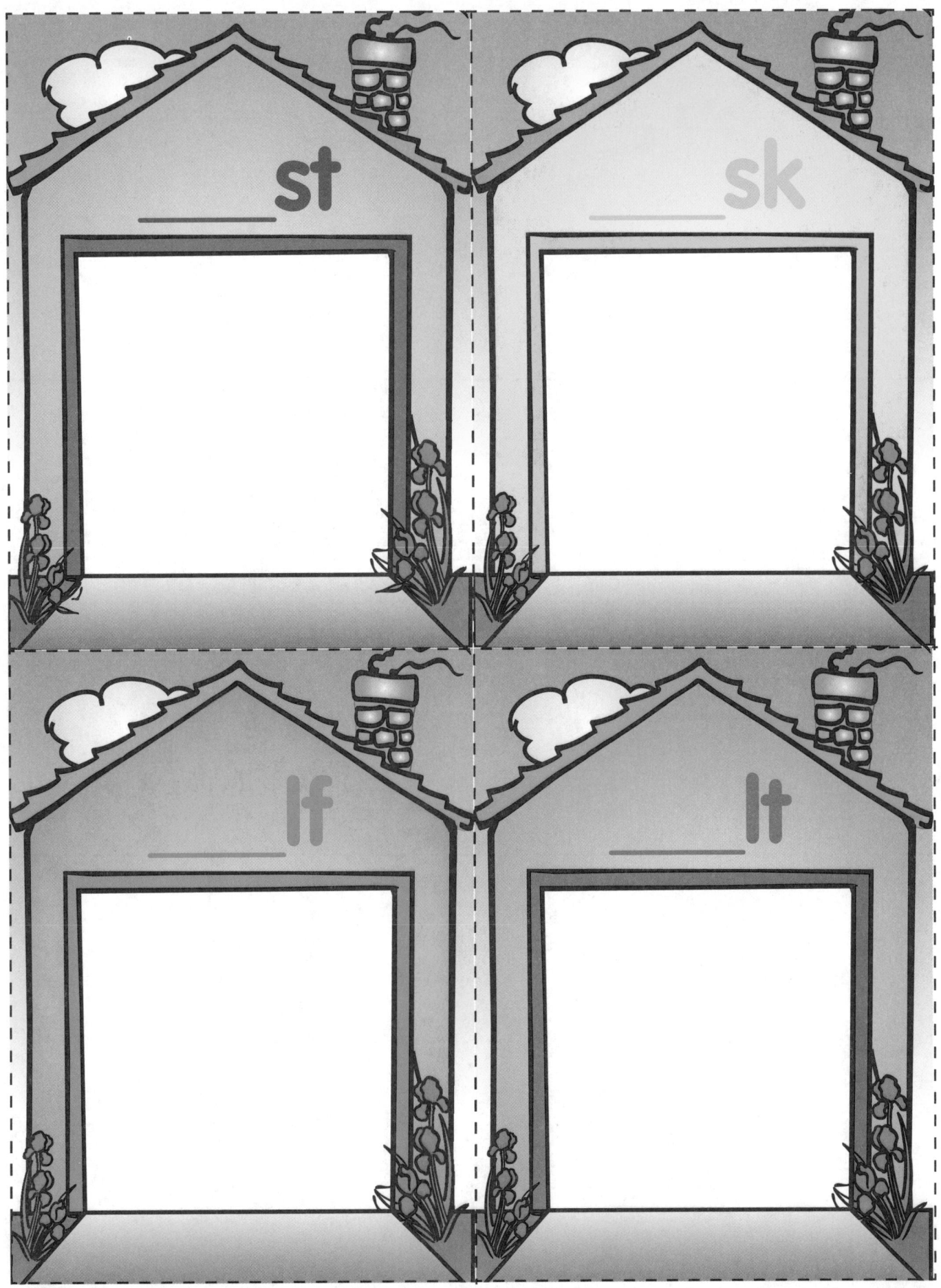

_____st

_____sk

_____lf

_____lt

114

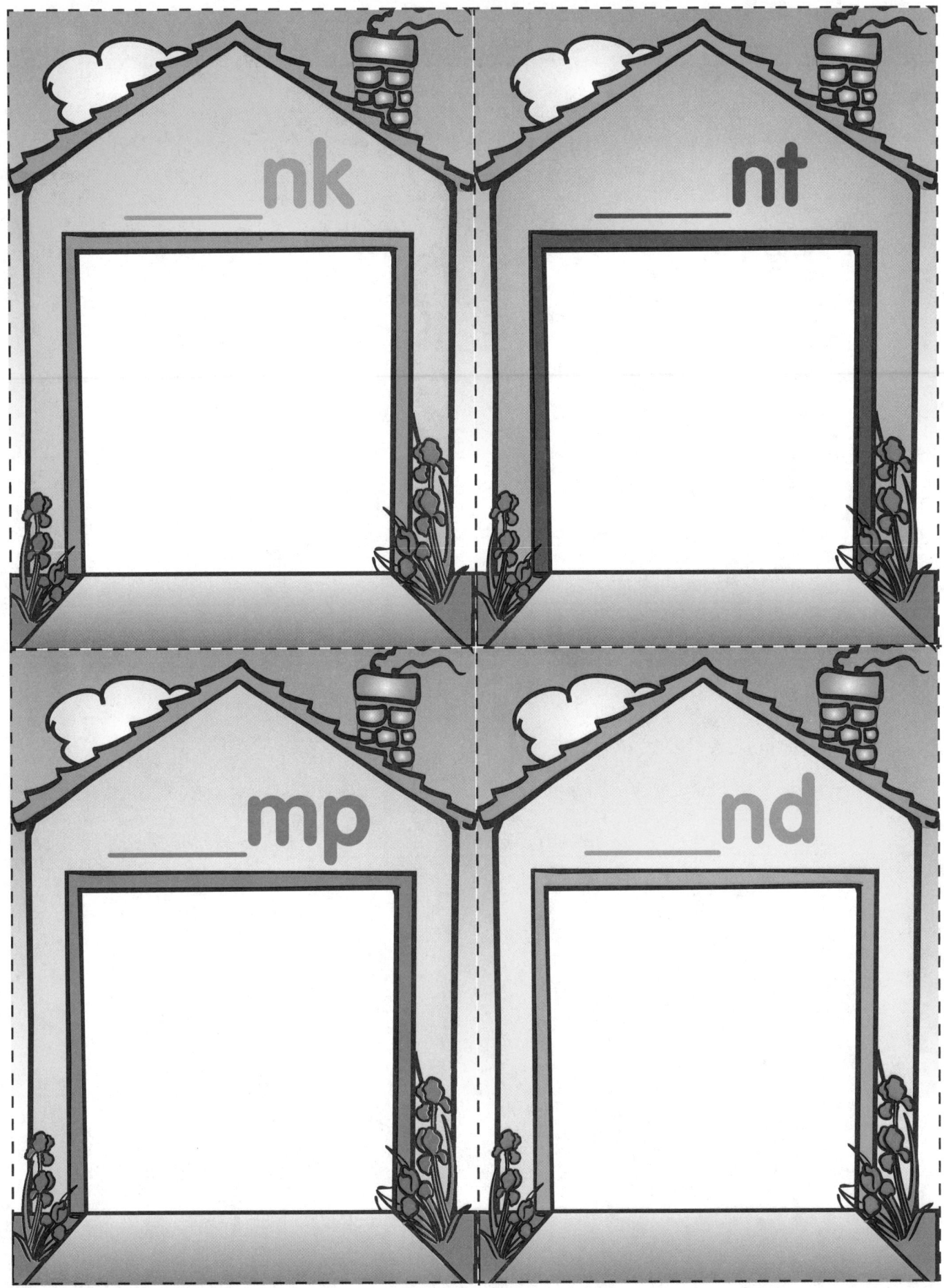

_____nk

_____nt

_____mp

_____nd

116

Listen to the End

Draw a picture that ends with the sound.

–st	–sk
–lf	–lt
–nk	–nt
–mp	–nd

Count the Parts

Skill: Syllables

Preparing the Center

1. Prepare an envelope following the directions on page 3.

   Cover—page 123
   Student Directions—page 125
   Sorting Labels—page 127
   Task Cards—pages 129–135

2. Reproduce a supply of the student activity sheet on page 137.

3. Place all center materials in the envelope.

Using the Center

In a Small Group

Place the labels faceup in a row on a flat surface. Place the picture cards in a small bag or box. One at a time, students draw a card and name the picture. The group decides how many syllables the word contains. The student who drew the card places the picture below the correct label. Students take turns drawing cards until the bag is empty.

Independently

The student sorts the picture cards by number of syllables, placing each picture below the correct label.

On the activity sheet, the student names the picture and circles the number of parts it contains.

Self-Checking Key

The back of each picture card shows the correct number of syllables in the word.

Count the Parts

I count 2 parts

tur·tle

zebra

flower

ball

124

Count the Parts

1. Take the labels and the cards out of the envelope.

2. Take each card and name the picture.

3. Count the number of parts in the name.

4. Place each card below the correct label.

5. Turn over the cards to check your answers.

6. Complete the activity sheet.

Skill: Syllables

goat

lamb

snail

dog

fly

hat

truck

box

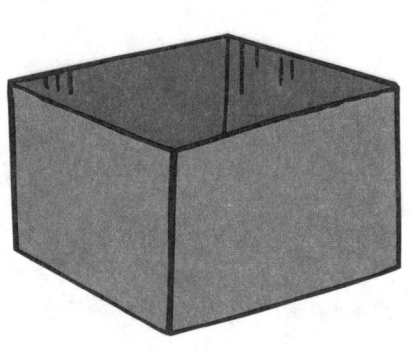

1

1

1

1

1

1

1

1

 monkey

 guitar

 lion

 flower

 bunny

 balloon

baby

 carrot

©2004 by Evan-Moor Corp.
Take It to Your Seat—Phonics Centers
EMC 3329

©2004 by Evan-Moor Corp.
Take It to Your Seat—Phonics Centers
EMC 3329

©2004 by Evan-Moor Corp.
Take It to Your Seat—Phonics Centers
EMC 3329

©2004 by Evan-Moor Corp.
Take It to Your Seat—Phonics Centers
EMC 3329

©2004 by Evan-Moor Corp.
Take It to Your Seat—Phonics Centers
EMC 3329

©2004 by Evan-Moor Corp.
Take It to Your Seat—Phonics Centers
EMC 3329

©2004 by Evan-Moor Corp.
Take It to Your Seat—Phonics Centers
EMC 3329

©2004 by Evan-Moor Corp.
Take It to Your Seat—Phonics Centers
EMC 3329

hamburger

computer

elephant

octopus

dinosaur

uniform

sunflower

grasshopper

©2004 by Evan-Moor Corp.
Take It to Your Seat—Phonics Centers
EMC 3329

©2004 by Evan-Moor Corp.
Take It to Your Seat—Phonics Centers
EMC 3329

©2004 by Evan-Moor Corp.
Take It to Your Seat—Phonics Centers
EMC 3329

©2004 by Evan-Moor Corp.
Take It to Your Seat—Phonics Centers
EMC 3329

©2004 by Evan-Moor Corp.
Take It to Your Seat—Phonics Centers
EMC 3329

©2004 by Evan-Moor Corp.
Take It to Your Seat—Phonics Centers
EMC 3329

©2004 by Evan-Moor Corp.
Take It to Your Seat—Phonics Centers
EMC 3329

©2004 by Evan-Moor Corp.
Take It to Your Seat—Phonics Centers
EMC 3329

alligator

helicopter

watermelon

rhinoceros

television

motorcycle

convertible

thermometer

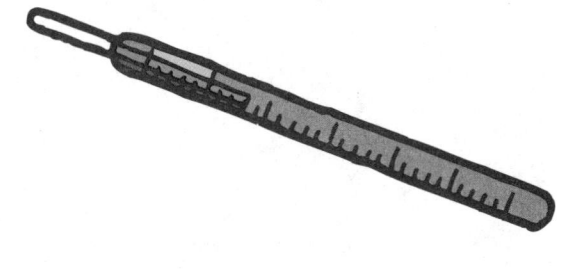

4

©2004 by Evan-Moor Corp.
Take It to Your Seat—Phonics Centers
EMC 3329

4

©2004 by Evan-Moor Corp.
Take It to Your Seat—Phonics Centers
EMC 3329

4

©2004 by Evan-Moor Corp.
Take It to Your Seat—Phonics Centers
EMC 3329

4

©2004 by Evan-Moor Corp.
Take It to Your Seat—Phonics Centers
EMC 3329

4

©2004 by Evan-Moor Corp.
Take It to Your Seat—Phonics Centers
EMC 3329

4

©2004 by Evan-Moor Corp.
Take It to Your Seat—Phonics Centers
EMC 3329

4

©2004 by Evan-Moor Corp.
Take It to Your Seat—Phonics Centers
EMC 3329

4

©2004 by Evan-Moor Corp.
Take It to Your Seat—Phonics Centers
EMC 3329

Count the Parts

Name the picture. Circle the number of parts.

1   2   3   4

1   2   3   4

1   2   3   4

1   2   3   4

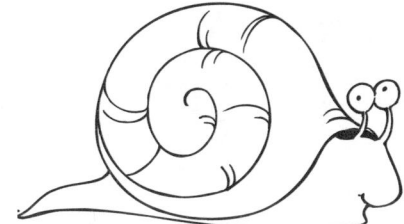

1   2   3   4

1   2   3   4

1   2   3   4

1   2   3   4

1   2   3   4

1   2   3   4

1   2   3   4

1   2   3   4

Word Family Fun

Skill: Word Families

Preparing the Center

1. Prepare an envelope following the directions on page 3.
   - Cover—page 139
   - Student Directions—page 141
   - Sorting Mats—pages 143–147
   - Task Cards—pages 149–153
2. Reproduce a supply of the student activity sheet on page 155.
3. Place all center materials in the envelope.

Using the Center

In a Small Group

Lay the sorting mats faceup on a flat surface. Place the word cards faceup nearby. Have students take turns choosing a word card, reading the word, and deciding in which word family it belongs. Continue until all word cards have been placed.

Independently

The student places the word cards on the correct sorting mats. The student then completes the activity sheet by writing the words in the correct boxes.

Self-Checking Key

The back of each word card has a shape the same color as its word family sorting mat.

Word Family Fun

_____ight

tight

knight

140

Word Family Fun

1. Choose a card. Read the word.

2. Place the card on the correct mat.

3. Find the correct mat for each of the words.

4. Turn over the cards to check your answers.

5. Complete the activity sheet.

Skill: Word Families

142

oat

_____

one

_____

ight

ide

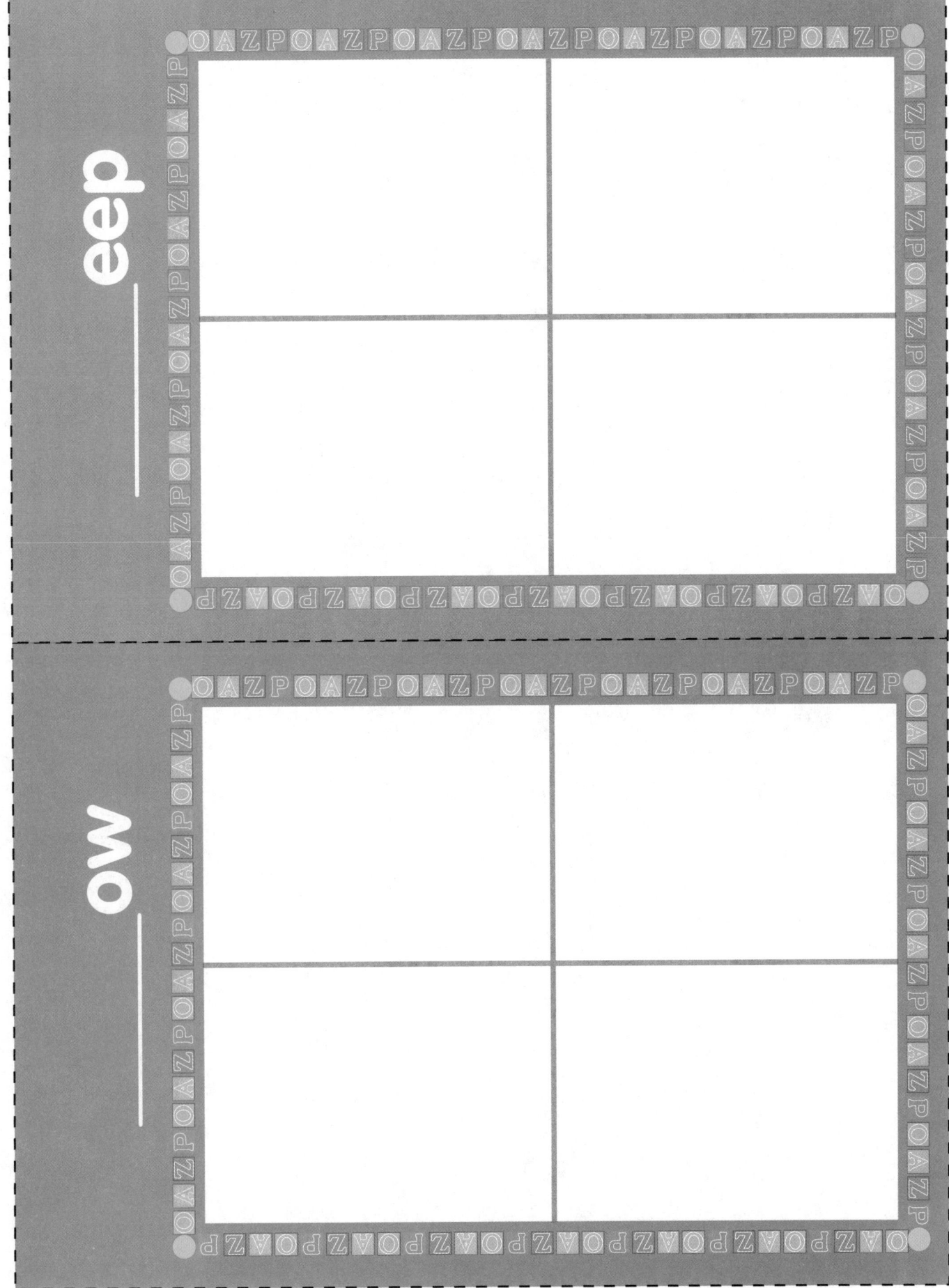

eep ___

ow ___

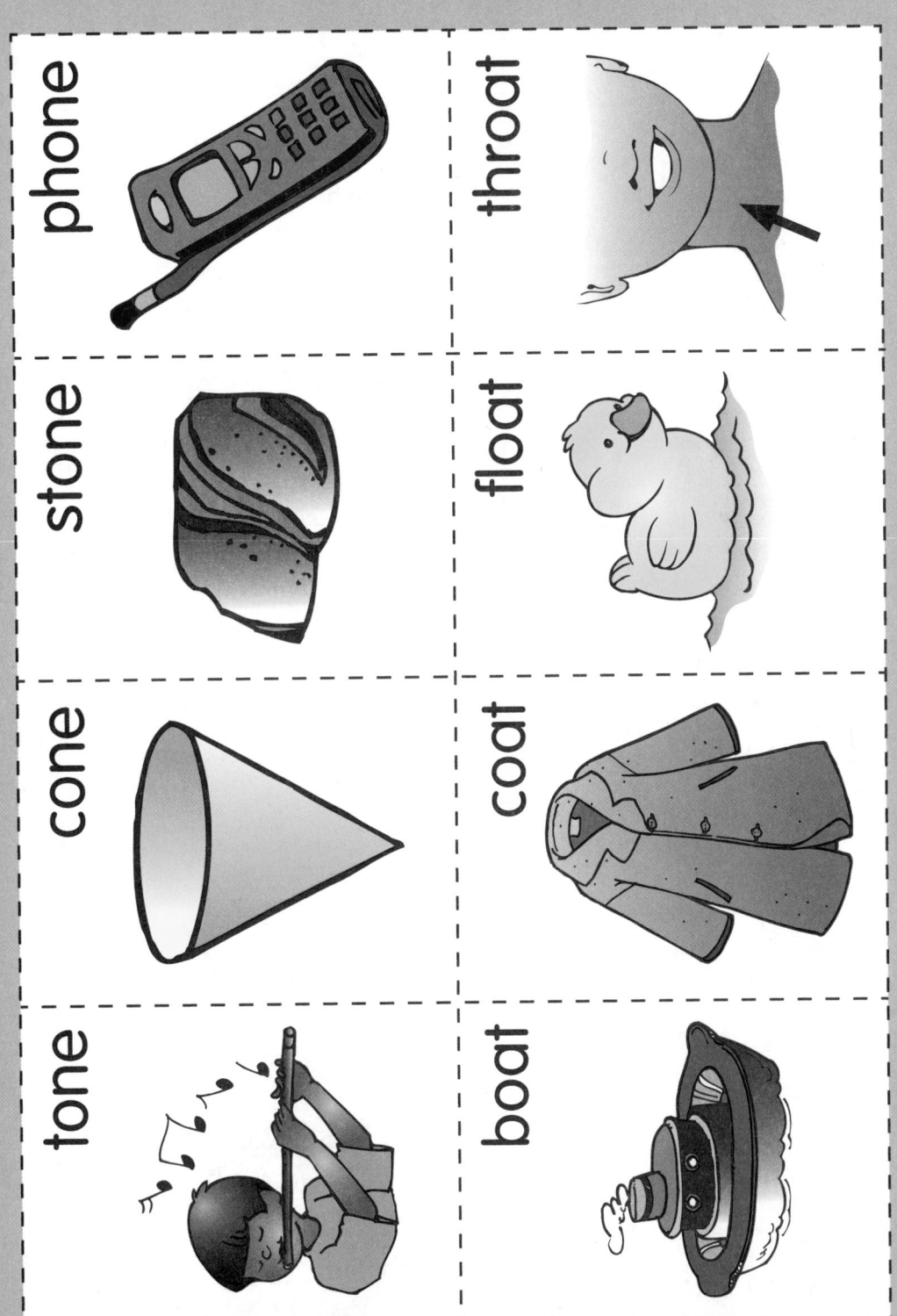

phone

throat

stone

float

cone

coat

tone

boat

bride

night

pride

light

ride

tight

hide

knight

151

bow

sheep

mow

sweep

row

sleep

snow

beep

Word Family Fun

Copy the words from the sorting mats in the correct boxes.

_____oat	_____one	_____ow

_____eep	_____ight	_____ide

Make a Word

Skill: Word Families

Preparing the Center

1. Prepare an envelope following the directions on page 3.
   Cover—page 157
   Student Directions—page 159
   Task Cards—pages 161 and 163
   Letter Cards—page 165
2. Reproduce a supply of the student activity sheet on page 167.
3. Place all center materials in the envelope.

Using the Center

In a Small Group

Place all of the letter cards faceup on a flat surface. Show one task card. Ask students to find letters that can be placed on the card to complete the three words. Then have the group read the word family they have made.

Repeat the steps with each card, or ask each student to take a card and build a word family to share with the group.

Independently

The student uses the letter cards to build word families on the task cards. Encourage the student to do several of the word families.

The student adds initial consonants to complete word families on the activity sheet.

Self-Checking Key

The back of each task card lists all the possible words for the word family that can be made using the available letters.

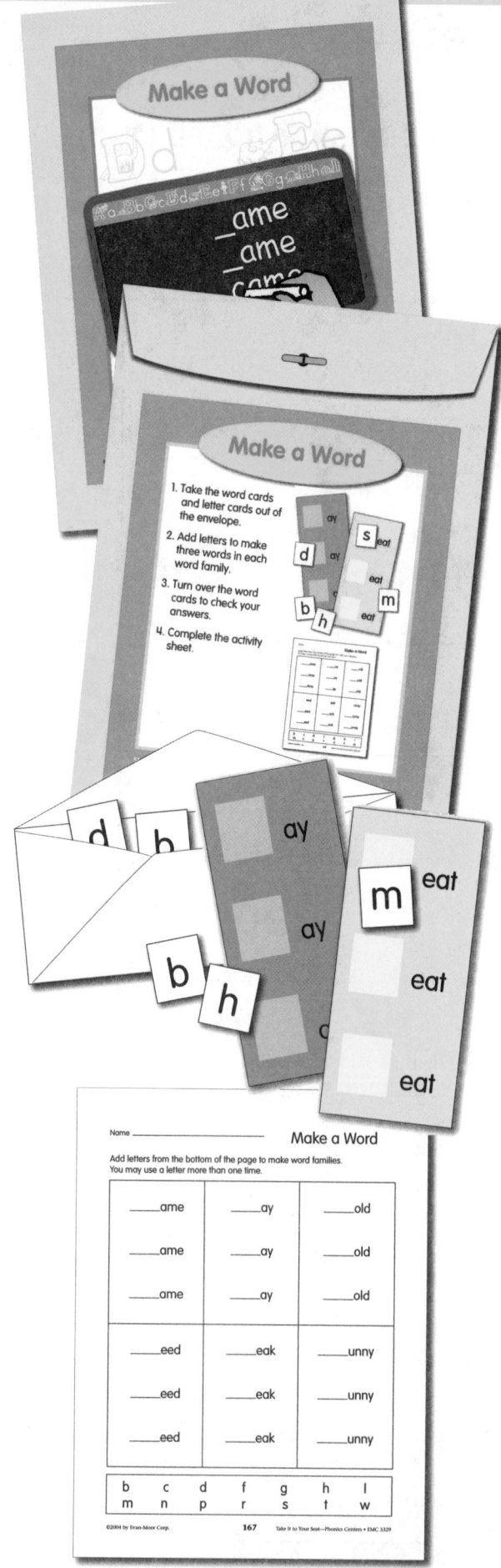

Make a Word

_ame

_ame

_ame

158

Make a Word

1. Take the word cards and letter cards out of the envelope.

2. Add letters to make three words in each word family.

3. Turn over the word cards to check your answers.

4. Complete the activity sheet.

Skill: Word Families

160

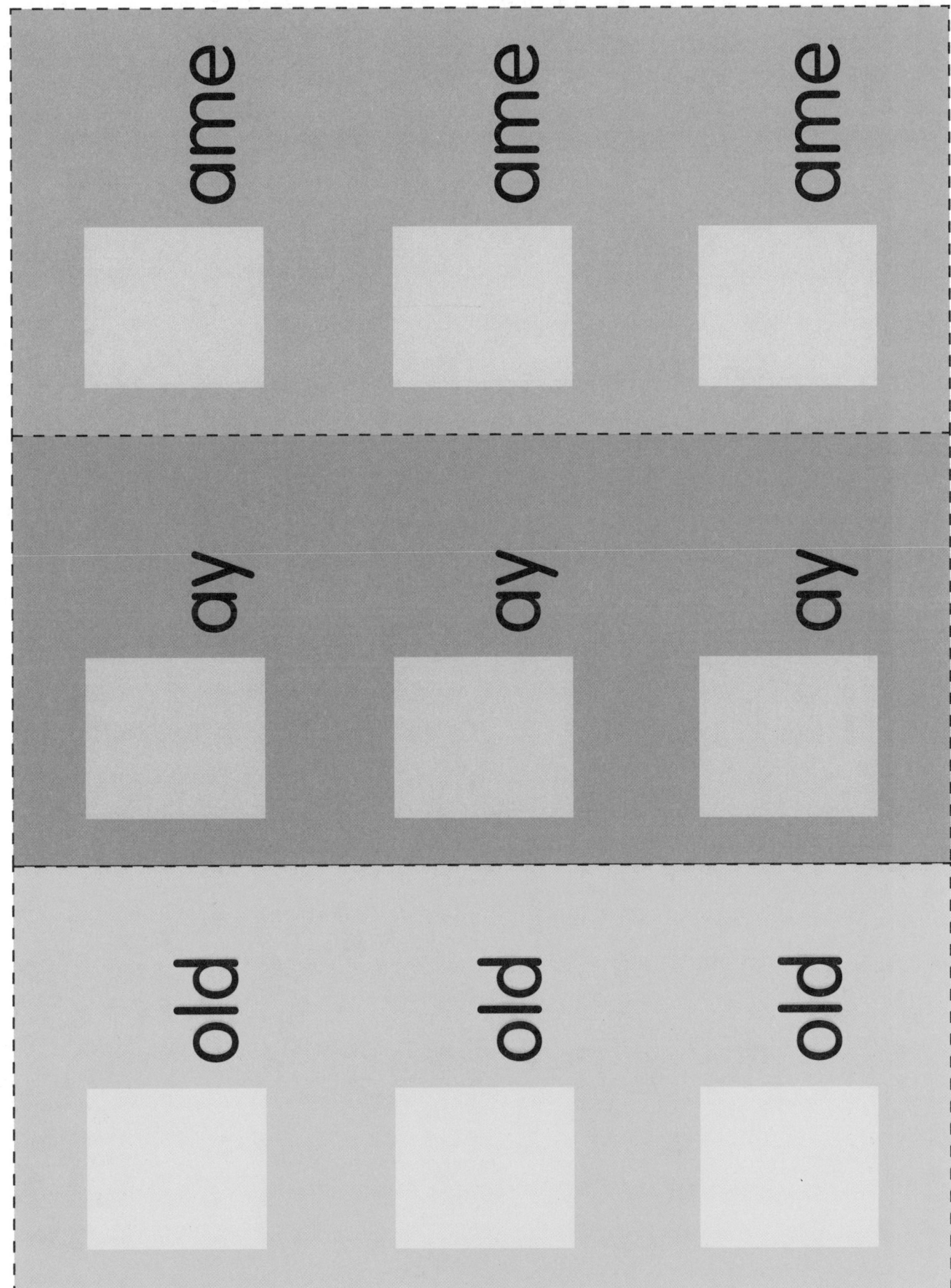

ame

ame

ame

ay

ay

ay

old

old

old

_ame

came
fame
game
lame
name
same
tame

_ay

bay
day
hay
jay
lay
may
pay
ray
way

_old

bold
cold
fold
gold
hold
mold
sold
told

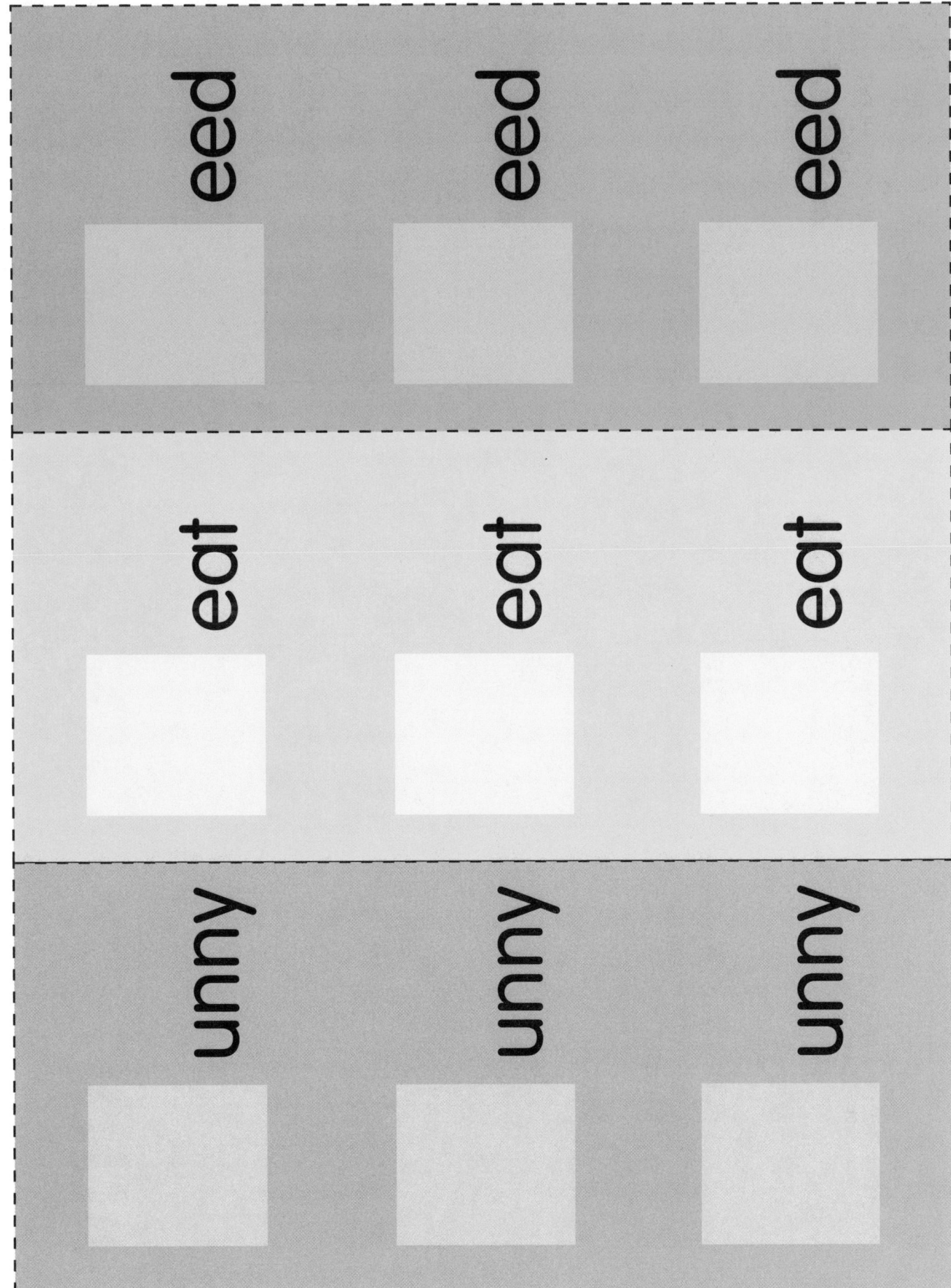

eed

eed

eed

eat

eat

eat

unny

unny

unny

163

_eed

deed
feed
heed
need
reed
seed
weed

_eat

beat
feat
heat
meat
neat
peat
seat

_unny

bunny
funny
runny
sunny

164

b	b	b	b	c	c
d	d	f	f	f	f
f	g	g	h	h	h
h	j	l	l	m	m
m	n	n	n	p	p
r	r	r	s	s	s
s	s	t	t	w	w

166

Make a Word

Add letters from the bottom of the page to make word families.
You may use a letter more than one time.

_____ame	_____ay	_____old
_____ame	_____ay	_____old
_____ame	_____ay	_____old
_____eed	_____eak	_____unny
_____eed	_____eak	_____unny
_____eed	_____eak	_____unny

b	c	d	f	g	h	l
m	n	p	r	s	t	w

Sounds of Y

Skill: Sounds of Final *y*

Preparing the Center

1. Prepare an envelope following the directions on page 3.
   Cover—page 169
   Student Directions—page 171
   Sorting Pockets—page 173
   Task Cards—page 175
2. Reproduce a supply of the student activity sheet on page 177.
3. Place all center materials in the envelope.

Using the Center

In a Small Group

Lay the sorting pockets faceup on a flat surface. Place the word cards in a small bag or box. Have students take turns choosing a card, reading the word, and deciding if the final *y* sounds like *e* or *i*. The word card is placed in the correct pocket.

Independently

The student reads the word cards and places them in the correct pocket to show the ending sounds for the letter *y*.

The student then completes the activity sheet by writing words in the correct boxes.

Self-Checking Key

The back of each word card has the letter *e* or *i* to represent the sound of *y*.

Sounds of Y

my

cry

Y I say i

silly

family

Y I say e

170

Sounds of Y

1. Take the pockets and cards out of the envelope.

2. Read each word card. Listen to the ending sound.

3. Put the cards in the correct pockets.

4. Turn over the cards to check your answers.

5. Complete the activity sheet.

Skill: Sounds of Final *y*

172

fold

cut

fold

173

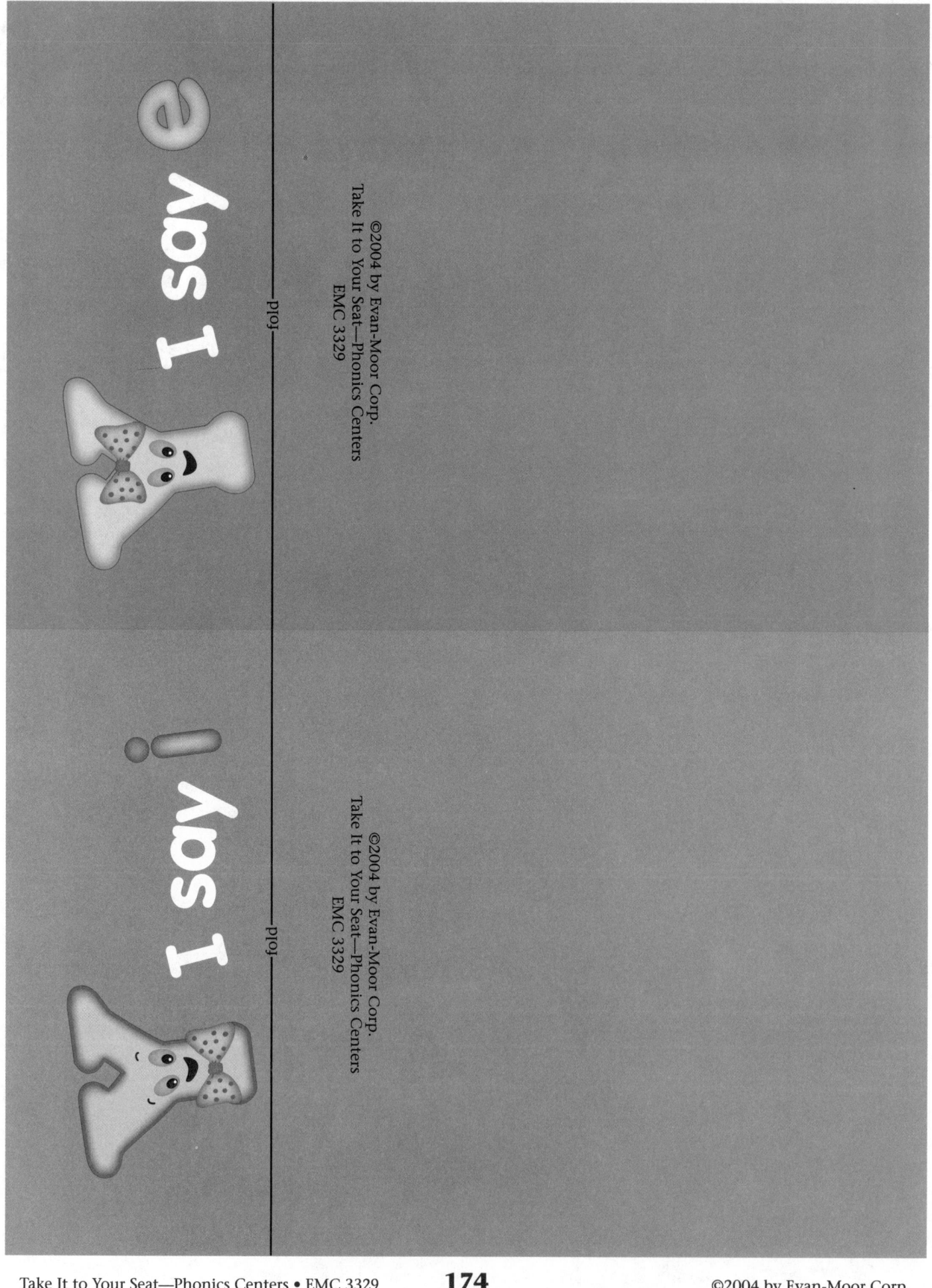

I say e

I say i

I say i

I say i

fold

fold

cry	try	shy	why
dry	my	spy	fry
lady	family	funny	any
tiny	sunny	silly	baby

 Take It to Your Seat—Phonics Centers • EMC 3329

i

i

i

i

i

i

i

i

e

e

e

e

e

e

e

e

Sounds of Y

Copy the word cards in each pocket in the correct box.

y says e bunny	y says i fly
1. _____	1. _____
2. _____	2. _____
3. _____	3. _____
4. _____	4. _____
5. _____	5. _____
6. _____	6. _____
7. _____	7. _____
8. _____	8. _____

The Right Word

Skill: Inflectional Endings

Preparing the Center

1. Prepare an envelope following the directions on page 3.
   - Cover—page 179
   - Student Directions—page 181
   - Sentence and Word Cards—pages 183–189
2. Reproduce a supply of the student activity sheet on page 191.
3. Place all center materials in the envelope.

Using the Center

In a Small Group

Place one sentence card and its three word cards faceup on a flat surface. Ask for a volunteer to read the first sentence. Students then decide which of the word cards correctly completes the sentence. Follow the same steps to complete the remaining two sentences.

Select another set of sentences and words and repeat the steps with the whole group.

Independently

Working with one set at a time, the student finds the correct words to complete each sentence. The student then writes the answers on the activity sheet.

Self-Checking Key

The back of each word card has a number showing which sentence it answers.

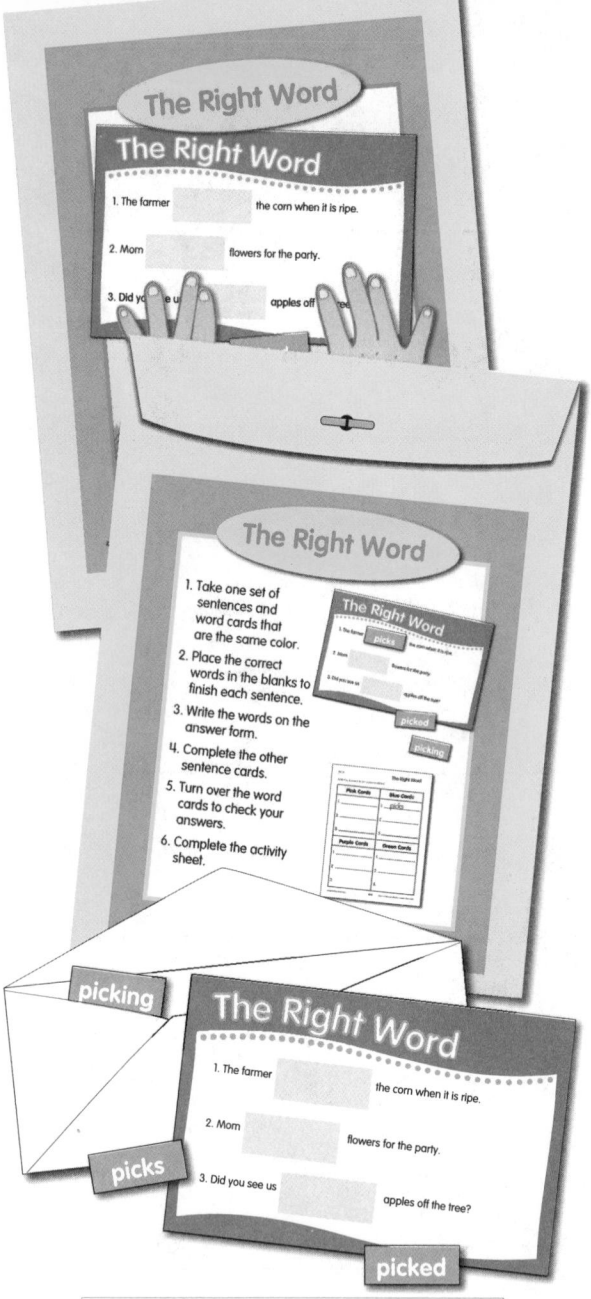

The Right Word

The Right Word

1. The farmer _____ the corn when it is ripe.

2. Mom _____ flowers for the party.

3. Did yo___ ___e u___ _____ apples off ___ree

picked

picking

picks

180

The Right Word

1. Take one set of sentences and word cards that are the same color.

2. Place the correct words in the blanks to finish each sentence.

3. Write the words on the answer form.

4. Complete the other sentence cards.

5. Turn over the word cards to check your answers.

6. Complete the activity sheet.

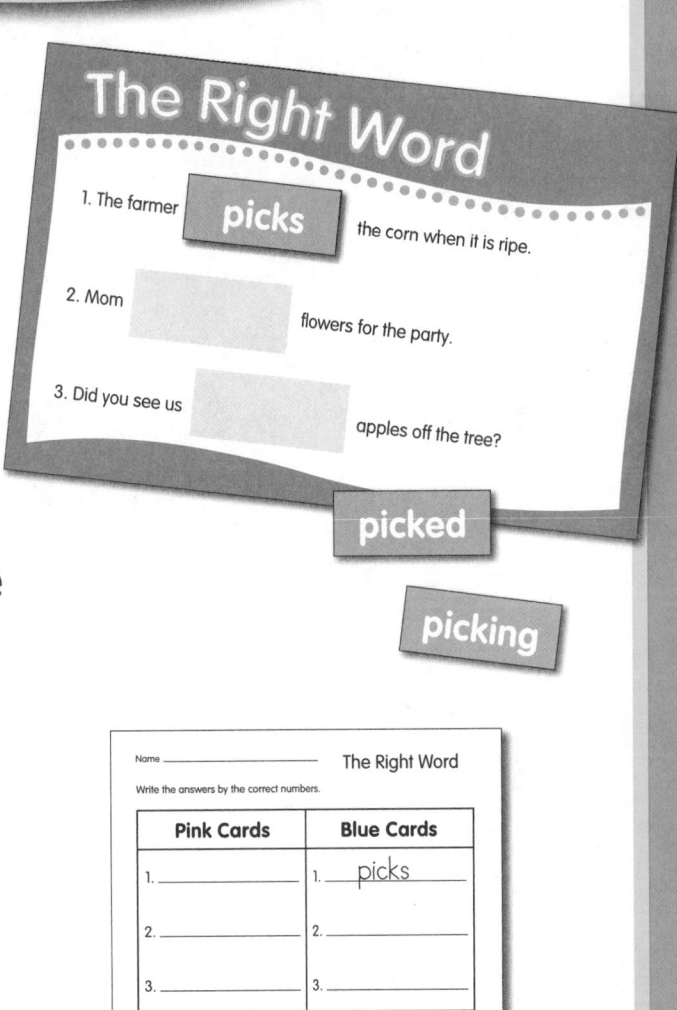

Skill: Inflectional Endings

182

The Right Word

1. She wants to _____ the piano.

2. They are _____ for the test.

3. He _____ his spelling words.

studying

studied

study

②

③

①

The Right Word

1. Bill is _____ to the ball field.

2. Every Saturday, Ann _____ to the library.

3. Yesterday, Kim _____ to the park.

walked

walks

walking

185

③

②

①

The Right Word

1. The farmer _____ the corn when it is ripe.

2. Mom _____ flowers for the party.

3. Did you see us _____ apples off the tree?

picking

picked

picks

187

③

②

①

The Right Word

1. Everybody _____ at the funny clown.

2. My little sister _____ when I make funny faces.

3. Do you _____ when you hear a joke?

laugh

laughs

laughed

189

③

②

①

190

The Right Word

Write the answers by the correct numbers.

Pink Cards

1. _____

2. _____

3. _____

Blue Cards

1. _____

2. _____

3. _____

Purple Cards

1. _____

2. _____

3. _____

Green Cards

1. _____

2. _____

3. _____

Answer Key

Page 21
Green cards (oval)
short/long **a:** bat, came
     e: red, jeep
     i: six, like
     o: fox, nose
     u: but, cute

Purple cards (triangle)
short/long **a:** and, rake
     e: men, see
     i: him, five
     o: not, most
     u: run, mule

Blue cards (rectangle)
short/long **a:** had, made
     e: get, need
     i: in, vine
     o: on, note
     u: bus, cube

Page 43

Name _____ What's My Vowel Sound?
Name the picture. Circle the vowel sound you hear.

Page 61

snail	suit	bow	glue
pie	leaf	jay	boat
jeep	tie	snow	light

Page 75
hard c:
cane
corn
comb
coat
cap
picnic

soft c:
celery
city
fence
face
mice
pencil

hard g:
gate
guitar
gift
gum
flag
frog

soft g:
gem
giraffe
gingerbread
general
gypsy
pigeon

Page 91

whale	sheep	cherry
teeth	shell	watch
thirty	fish	wheel
thumb	bench	whistle

Page 107

star	skunk	flag
dragon	frog	clown
crab	grapes	plant

Page 121
Pictures will vary, but must contain the correct ending blend.

Page 137

Name _____ Count the Parts
Name the picture. Circle the number of parts.

©2004 by Evan-Moor Corp. 137 Take It to Your Seat—Phonics Centers • EMC 3329

Page 155

_one:	**_oat:**
bone	boat
cone	coat
phone	float
stone	throat

_ide:	**_ight:**
hide	knight
ride	tight
pride	light
bride	night

_ow:	**_eep:**
snow	beep
mow	sleep
row	sweep
bow	sheep